2/14/07

Sister Carter,

May God watch over you...
You are truly a blessing.

God Bless!
De Lóna

SPIRITUAL LESSONS FOR MY SISTERS

ALSO BY NATASHA MUNSON

Life Lessons for My Sisters

SPIRITUAL LESSONS FOR MY SISTERS

Natasha Munson

*How to Get Over the Drama
and Live Your Best Life!*

HYPERION

NEW YORK

Library of Congress Cataloging-in-Publication Data
Munson, Natasha.
 Spiritual lessons for my sisters : how to get over the drama and live your best life! /
Natasha Munson.— 1st ed.
  p. cm.
 ISBN 1-4013-0806-6 (pbk.)
  1. African American women—Religious life. 2. African American women—
Conduct of life. 3. Self-realization—Religious aspects. I. Title.
BL625.2.M76 2005
248.8'43'08996073—dc22   2004062551

Hyperion books are available for special promotions and premiums. For details contact Michael Rentas, Assistant Director, Inventory Operations, Hyperion, 77 West 66th Street, 12th floor, New York, New York 10023, or call 212-456-0133.

FIRST EDITION

10 9 8 7 6 5 4 3 2 1

I dedicate this book to all the spirits who have encountered their own form of hell and lived to get through it, smile, and find their own paradise. To all the men and women who have been violated but still learned to trust and love fully. And to all of those who thought that one decision would change the course of their life and then found out that they still had choices, still had a life they could create, still had God, and could still love and dream   again and again.

ACKNOWLEDGMENTS

THANK YOU TO EVERY PERSON who has been a part of my spiritual journey. I thank you for your love, friendship, inspiration, encouragement, and wisdom.

Thank you to Bob Miller, Kelly Notaras, David Dunton, Jane Comin, Ellen Archer, Beth Dickey, Charlie Davidson, and everyone at Hyperion and Harvey Klinger, Inc., for having faith in my work, for being an inspiration, for comforting me when my travel plans get chaotic, and for being authentically good people. Thank you for all you have done to make my work successful. Susan Driscoll for always providing advice and encouragement. iUniverse for continuously including me in their stories of success. My readers for touching my heart with every e-mail you send. Thank you for your prayers and support. To every person who took a chance on an aspiring author, I appreciate your time, faith, and energy.

To family and friends and those in between, thank you for teaching me a lesson and being a part of my life.

As a teenager I used to sit in my room with tears in my eyes and hum a few lines from a song that always reminded me that things would get easier and much brighter. Thank you, God, for taking me through the pain and bringing me to a point where I love my life so very much. I am grateful to have my life experiences used for inspiration and encouragement. I am so very grateful for every person who reads my work and experiences his or her own moment of knowing things will get better, starting right now.

CONTENTS

INTRODUCTION

SPIRITUAL LESSONS began as a way for me to believe in the possibilities of life and love again. I wanted so much to believe in living a life I loved. I wanted to look in the mirror and find a way to truly love myself again. When I wrote my first book, *Life Lessons for My Sisters*, I subtitled it *How to Make Wise Choices and Live a Life You Love!* I was showing young women how to make the choices I had not made. I was telling them to do the opposite of what I had done up to that point. Because, when I wrote the book, I was not living a life I loved. But I knew it was possible. And so I wrote down everything I wished I had done. I wrote the lessons God gave me after painful moments in my life. And I saw that living a life I loved was not a fantasy. It was possible!

In order to get there, though, you have to shed everything. You have to go within yourself and look at yourself honestly. You have to look at everything you've been through and everything you've endured, and you have to love yourself in spite of and because of all of that. You have to realize that no matter where you are in life, you should never give up on yourself. No matter how frustrated you are, no matter how many problems you are dealing with, even if you feel like ending it all, there is always an alternative. You just have to be willing to believe. You have to have faith that a better life exists. And then you have to take the steps to create the life you really want.

Remove yourself from the barrage of issues, obstacles, negative people, bad environments, thoughts of doubt and fear, and take yourself to the next level. *Life Lessons* gave me a glimmer of what was possible in my life. *Spiritual Lessons* is the next level—the level where I'm no longer wishing for a better life. I'm no longer hoping that your life is better than the hell I was dealing with when I initially wrote *Life Lessons. Spiritual Lessons* is authentically me. It is what I have endured. It is what I have become. It is who I am.

I woke up once in the middle of the night and realized that I was smiling in my sleep—smiling from my soul! It was then that I knew that we always get through our painful moments. If we take a step toward greatness, God will be with us every step of the way.

Thank you for taking this journey with me. I love my life. I love who I am, and I hope to help you to be able to do the same.

Live a life you love!

You control your thoughts.
Your thoughts determine your actions.
Your actions create your life.

BE HONEST WITH YOURSELF

In the beginning of the year, many people begin writing down their goals and resolutions. People make promises and say proudly to themselves, "This is my year." The sad truth is that most of these people, including you, will not achieve these goals. You won't stick to your resolutions. You won't stick to your diet or budget. When the year ends you will either be in the same place you were in last year or just a step ahead or behind. So the real question is, what are you going to do about your life?

Almost every publication begins their January issue with diet and financial planning information. And you know why these things sell year after year—because 95 percent of the population is going to need the same information next year. Can you honestly say you're willing to do whatever it takes to change your life this year? Can you really say that you will do everything you possibly can to change your financial, spiritual, and emotional life? Or are you more talk than action?

I don't mean to be hard on you, but I don't want to be easy on you, or myself, either. I don't want us to go into cheerleader mode unless we are actually committed to winning the game.

So before you sit down to write out your goals, be honest with yourself. Assess your strengths and weaknesses. Stop the BS—Blocking your Spirit—this year. Stop lying to yourself. Stop wasting your precious time and stop wasting the life God gave you. We have to stop misusing our energy and begin to focus on the things we really want. The Bible says whatsoever a man thinketh, so he shall become. I encourage you to change the way you have been thinking. Stop doing the things that have been hindering your progress. Stop wishing for a better life and get out there and create it. Focus on the solutions. Focus on the opportunities. Focus on the blessings. Focus on learning more and enriching your life financially.

If you are ready to commit to living your best life this year, then you must:

> *Be honest with yourself*
> *Be committed to your happiness*
> *Be prepared to work to create your financial freedom*
> *Be open to the opportunities*
> *Live from a position of power*
> *Stop looking at the obstacles*
> *Realize that everything works in your favor, everything works out exactly the way you think it will*
> *Think differently*
> *Stop saying "I wish" and start claiming your blessings beforehand*
> *Create an "I Have . . . I Am" mentality*

LESSON

Life changes when you commit to doing what is necessary to create a life you love.

HOW DID I GET HERE?

Have you ever sat down, thought about your life, cried, and said, "How did I get here?" Have you had a moment when you want to sing the lyrics to an Erykah Badu song? Maybe I made a wrong turn back there somewhere. If you have a relationship with God, you will go through times of struggle. You will experience times that make you question your sanity. You will wonder how you got "here." You will question your choices and feel stuck and stagnant in your life. All of these thoughts are blessings. Yes, they are amazing blessings.

When you are experiencing a time of trouble or stress, you are being called upon to remember the good times. When you are experiencing a time of financial difficulty, you are being called upon to remember the many times God gave you more than enough. Whenever you experience a loss, you are being called upon to remember that you were blessed to have that spirit in your life.

Wherever you are in life, be grateful. Be thankful. Be happy with all the moments of your life. Regardless of what's going on in your life right now, things could be worse. You may not realize it, but every moment that you are here, you are being blessed and prepared. Appreciate the fact that God noticed your life and is testing you to see if you will seek greatness.

You see, if you didn't deserve more, you wouldn't have those days of wondering, What did I do with my life? If God wasn't getting you ready to receive more, you wouldn't have moments of pain and difficulty. You are being prepared to appreciate the joy and love in your life. But how will you ever truly appreciate these things if you don't know the alternative?

In order to know love, at some point you had to know pain. In order to laugh out loud, you had to know sadness. In order to rejoice and be grateful, you had to deal with some difficulty.

We all experience moments of wonderment about our life. The goal is to know that we are in the right place. We have to appreciate this moment—the good and the bad.

LESSON

Each day write down the reasons you should be grateful and the goals that make living your life worthwhile.

DO YOU TRUST YOURSELF?

The best way to find out if someone deserves to be in your life is to ask him or her, "Do you trust yourself?"

If you have no trust in yourself, you have no strong faith in God; you have no belief in your capabilities. Why would anyone trust someone who doesn't even trust him- or herself?

So many times we bring people into our world who are not capable of giving us any spiritual nourishment, any knowledge, any peace, any enhancements. They simply are leeches of our time, energy, and, sometimes, love.

When you acknowledge your connection to God and can truly rely on your intuition and the way your spirit reacts to situations, you are powerful. Because of that, people must be worthy to be in the presence of God that exists within you.

Do not sell yourself short. Do not sell God short. God created this world for you. You are here to live, love, learn, and share. If you have people in your life who are not doing that, if you are not doing that, then you are not totally on your path. You have to reconnect, seek God, and he shall seek you.

The best consolation doesn't come from having a friend to provide advice or a good book to turn to. It is about tuning in to our spirit and listening as God tells us what to do. There is no greater connection to God than one-on-one communication.

Talk to God. Listen to your spirit. Don't allow anyone to keep you off the path to greatness.

When someone does not trust himself or herself, they do

not trust the universe or the power of God. They have stronger faith in what man can create or destroy. They do not truly believe that what God has put together, no man can break.

When you have listened to your intuition and talked to God, you will only attract people who are of God, and those will be the ones who will become your friends.

Treat yourself well. Love yourself. Empower yourself by listening to the God that is always and will forever be in *you*. Trust in yourself and ally yourself with those who trust themselves, for then you know, they trust God.

LESSON

You are powerful, and people must be worthy to be in the presence of God that exists within you.

STAND IN YOUR TRUTH

One thing you will always and forever have is your own truth. You can be empowered or limited by it. It is all within your choosing.

To align yourself with the needs of your spirit, you must first acknowledge your spirit. What do you need to feel whole? What do you need to feel as though you are doing something beneficial for yourself? What do you need to feel love in your heart and soul every day? What do you need to feel cherished?

The needs of your spirit are the most important and essential needs. Once you focus on fulfilling these needs, you will begin down a road to power and glory.

Through the many painful moments I have been through, I have always had two things—the strength of my spirit and the knowledge that "this too shall pass."

My firm belief that the pain would pass opened me up to knowing without a doubt that God would see me through, and therefore my faith does not waver. My God has my back. Any dream I have for myself pales in comparison to the dream God has for you and me.

To stand in your truth is to know when something or someone is not right for you. People do not just lie to you; you allow them to lie to you. If you keep someone in your life whom you do not fully trust, you are limiting yourself. If you allow someone to make excuses as to why they cannot do this or that, or spend time with you, you are limiting yourself to their needs, their inability to give.

You must know your limitations and boundaries. You have to know when someone is overstepping those boundaries with you. You have to know when someone is limiting you, hurting you, or just standing in the way of your blessings and love. You have to know when to tell them to get out of your life, so true love and friendship can come in.

One of the best gifts we can give to our children and ourselves is simply—stand in your truth. Live a life that fulfills you. Live a life that you love talking about. Live a life that makes you happy and joyful and keeps you with the ability to laugh. Be happy with who you are and how you are.

LESSON

People do not just lie to you; you allow them to lie to you.

SPEAK YOUR TRUTH

Many people will hide, run from, and deny hearing and acknowledging the truth, even when it stares them plainly and boldly in the face. There are some things we simply do not want to hear or say. We would rather hear a good excuse than hear the truth. And no matter how many times people mutter that they would appreciate the truth much more than an excuse or a lie, the truth of the matter is that most people would embrace a good lie rather than hear a truth that may change their world.

There are certain things we always know. We always know when something is right for us or not. We always know when someone is lying to us. We just tend not to listen to the truth our spirit tells us. To me, life is about going higher and higher—spiritually, financially, and emotionally. If we are to commit to that, then we must commit to speaking and living the truth. We must not hide behind or deny our truth. We must not shy away from telling the truth. We cannot create excuses and justifications for not telling the truth.

Jesus told Peter and Judas that they would betray him. He didn't talk about it behind their back. He didn't hide the fact that he knew their intentions. He called them out right on the spot. It wasn't malicious. It wasn't hurtful. It was the truth and he spoke it.

Speak your truth.

LESSON

We always know when something is right for us or not. We just tend not to listen to the truth our spirit tells us.

THE PATTERNS OF OUR LIVES

The reality of life is that so many people are unhappy. Without a belief in love, faith, hope for a better life, or understanding that they create their life, many people just go through life in a cyclical motion.

To make any real difference in your life, you must look at the patterns. Realize that if you always use the same actions, you will always achieve the same results. In order for life to change, you must have faith, hope, belief, and understanding.

Faith. In this moment, acknowledge that you are no better than anyone else. But you are powerful because God is within you. You cannot create a life you love unless you give the power of change over to God. You must know that with God you can make it through anything.

Belief. There is a big difference between wishing and knowing that you will achieve something. So many of us wish for the luxuries that come with success. So many are envious of people who have achieved success. But we are never envious of their process. We never understand or acknowledge the journey someone had to undertake to become powerful, spiritual, loving, and successful. We never want to know the full story, only the glory.

In order to achieve anything, you must look at the full picture. Know in your heart and soul that you can achieve. Do not judge yourself based on what someone else has done or achieved. Know what you are capable of. Know that God gave you a purpose. It is your duty to your spirit and to God to fulfill it.

Hope. If you want hope, you must see God before everything else. You must know that even with the pain, fear, and anger in the world, the first and last thing that exists is love. God is love. God is here, in your world, if you acknowledge God.

When you acknowledge God, hope is automatically instilled in your being. When you have hope, you can believe in others. You can believe in yourself. When you have hope, you know that one person, one spirit, can make a difference in the lives of others.

It is not about how many people you know, but how you touch the hearts of others.

Understanding. When you have the three elements of faith, hope, and belief, you become understanding of the world and its processes. You realize that everything happens for a reason.

Everything that happens, good or bad, needs to be acknowledged because it is meant to teach you. It is meant to push you farther along.

When you have understanding, you are open to listening. You will listen to your spirit. And you will listen to others without judging their life or motives.

Understanding gives you peace. Once you take away the need to judge others or to know their motivations and just realize that they are simply being all they can be at that moment, you are on your road to self-empowerment.

Life is about knowing that you are love, God is love, and

God is within you and everyone else. When you know this, then you can let go and just *be* you.

When you have understanding, you're not in wonderment or confusion. You are simply flowing with life and allowing others to be themselves. You are no longer taking on the problems of others because you understand that life is a process, and that everyone must learn in their own way, at their own pace.

Understand that life is a flowing process. And yes, you can control the direction, but you must know when to let the waves of life lead you to your best place.

Change the way you think about life. Get out of the mental entrapment of lost dreams, little faith, lack of trust, and disbelief. Know that at this moment this life is yours. You can create a life you love or you can simply exist.

Will your life continue to show the same patterns? Or will you embrace faith, hope, belief, and understanding, and create the powerful life that is meant to be yours?

LESSON

If you want love, you must give love.

If you want faith, you must have faith in others.

If you want to believe in the good of others, you must be good.

If you want to trust again, you must be trustworthy.

If you want success, you must help others.

ENDING A FRIENDSHIP?

———

Our spirit always knows what is right for us. Our spirit always guides us to the truth. Our spirit always tells us when something or someone is not right for us.

The reality is we do not listen. We tend to tune out our spirit and settle into the "comfort" of the friendship. We make excuses for the individual. We make excuses for the situation. We justify everything except the reason to terminate the relationship.

When you are out of alignment with your spirit, it is very difficult to make changes of any kind. It is especially difficult to acknowledge a growth in your spirit and the need to eliminate certain people from your life.

Our human side never wants to come off as "I'm better or beyond you." Yet sometimes we have moved beyond a relationship. Our spirit has allowed us to grow and our mind is holding us back.

Allow your spirit to guide you. Listen when God talks to you through your intuition. Listen when a person shows you how they really are. And listen when they tell you they are not right for you.

Then make a decision and stick to it. Push yourself to the next level.

You must constantly be in the process of learning and growing. Know when to eliminate anything that is affecting your mental energy and spirit.

As far as actually telling someone that you need to end your "friendship" with him or her, stand in your truth. Tell them how you feel and express your need for growth. Without placing guilt, making excuses, or creating ways to change it, explain your need to step away. Be certain that you are doing what is right for your spirit and do not fall into the needs of the other individual.

We often keep people in our lives just because we're used to them. Don't do this to yourself or allow anyone to do this to you. If you want to experience life and live it to its fullest, you must take control on all levels.

A lesson I have learned in regard to deteriorating friendships is that we are not obligated. We are not obligated to continue with friendships that are not nurturing to our spirit or good for our soul. We are not obligated to be someone's friend because they choose to be ours. We are not obligated to pretend to be friends just because we have been friends in the past. The lesson in life is that there are seasons of our lives. Some people will be with you for a lifetime. Some will only be in your life to share a lesson or two. The key is to know the difference and know when to move on. Know what your soul needs to feel nurtured and inspired. When you hold on to unfulfilling friendships and relationships, you are not giving your spirit the freedom and love it needs.

LESSON

Never misuse your time, energy, or love.

HOW DO I MAKE A CHANGE IN MY LIFE?

Listen. Before you attempt to make any change in your life, listen to your spirit. Tune out the voices of others and simply listen to the God within you. Our best advice comes from our most powerful connection to God, our intuition.

Prepare. Be prepared for change. Know how you will handle obstacles. Know what you want out of a situation. Know what you are prepared to give your time, energy, and love to. Be focused on your goal and stick to the advice God has given you. So many times we try to ignore our spirit or justify what our subconscious is telling us. If you stop debating with your spirit and simply listen and prepare for change, you will be able to make the necessary steps to change your life.

Plan. If we want to make any changes in life, we cannot sit and wait for the good to come to us. You have to make your future and create your destiny. Never give up on your dreams or goals, simply plan a way to get there and give yourself a time line and deadline.

Be Ready. You must have your spirit and mind prepared for the changes God will bring. Realize that the experiences life will bring are not always what you had planned or hoped for, but if you have the love of God and realize that you are powerful because God is within you, you will overcome every obstacle. Not only will you come out on the glorious side but you will also be a more powerful, spiritual, loving person if you remain a conscious participant in your life and look at how the lessons of your life unfold and shape you as a person.

Focus. No matter what occurs in your life, never lose sight of your goal. If you want to achieve, you must believe you can, ask and thank God for it, and then you must continue to work toward that goal on a daily basis.

LESSON

Our best advice comes from our most powerful connection to God, our intuition.

THE "WHY ME?" BLUES CHOIR

There are so many of us who sing in the "why me?" blues choir. We allow our troubles and problems to overwhelm us. We allow indecision to take us in its grip. We allow fear to make us stagnant. We allow the opinion of others to guide our life. We allow the painful experiences of our childhood to create our life.

We have to get out of the "why me?" syndrome and start to live life. We have to stop allowing negative experiences of the past to affect our present. Whether you dealt with a bad experience yesterday or ten years ago, you have to let it go. You have to forgive the person who affected you. You have to forgive yourself for allowing things to affect you today. You deserve forgiveness.

Let's move past all the painful experiences we have endured. Let's start going toward fulfilling spiritual experiences. Let's move forward together and see just how much joy, love, peace, and happiness God can give us. Let's start singing praises and eliminate the blues. It's time.

LESSON

You are not the only one who has experienced pain, but you can be one of the few to get over it and make your life glorious.

THE MOMENTS OF LIFE

———

I thought there were moments to be had
but as my life flashed before me
I realized that I had been given more than enough
time
to fulfill my dreams
I had just simply misused it
taken it for granted
not appreciated
the breaths
not appreciated
the moments
not appreciated the life
until it was flashing before me
then I could see the time that had been so available
then I saw the moments that were misused
then I saw the opportunities that had been missed
because of my lack of focus
then I saw that we are all given our proper time
What shall we do with our gift of time

What shall we do with this life
What will we do in the last breath
Will we sigh in appreciation of a life well lived
or will we cry and only wish
we had more time
more life
more moments to appreciate
Will we appreciate our existence
Will we have added anything to our life
Will we have added anything to our world
Will people still be talking about us days, weeks, and years
after our death
Will we have made an impact
Will we have changed someone's life for the better
Will we have loved
Will we have been loved
Will we have dreamed
and seen those dreams become a reality
When we realize that our world is spinning
will we have the strength to bring it back
Will we have the courage to control it
Will we ever appreciate who we are and how we are
or will we finally understand in our last moment
that this was it
this was the life we were supposed to love

In the end what will you do

Will you sigh or will you cry

in the end will you have lived

or just existed

in the end will you be missed

or will you become a distant memory

What are you doing today to show your appreciation

for your life

What are you doing today to make your dreams happen

What are you doing today to reach into life and claim your

space

What are you really doing?

ELIMINATE TOXIC PEOPLE

There comes a time during your spiritual journey when you become so overwhelmed, so filled by spirit, that you will truly know the meaning of being visited by the holy spirit.

As the thoughts raced through my mind I mentally tried to tune them out. My thoughts were emotional and irrational. But my spirit was listening. My spirit told me to take heed to the energies around me. I have taken great care to eliminate the negative energy around me. I don't tolerate or attract negative energy. So I have been living with this amazing sense of peace. And then, in the middle of the night, I awoke almost as if from a dream, and my spirit simply said, There is a difference between negative people and toxic people. You've eliminated the negative, it's time to go to the next level and eliminate the toxic people. You cannot move forward if there are energies in your life that are holding you back.

I felt like I had just been hit with a strong force of wisdom. I had just been given knowledge that my spirit needed, and it was so important that I receive and accept the message that I was prompted to wake up and be fully aware of these thoughts.

Toxic people are those people who enter our lives under the guise of being positive people. You misinterpret their actions and words and believe that they have the same heart and spirit you do. These people will talk about empowerment, making changes in their lives, about the good they want to do, they will even quote some scriptures, but they do not mean you well. Their energy, at the core, is toxic. Their inner thoughts of insecurity and disbelief can permeate your world if you allow it. Their ability to justify and make excuses for their lives can affect your choices and expectations of others, if you allow it.

In order to proceed on this spiritual journey, we're going to have to take a strong look at all the people that are around us, and the energy they bring. It's time to clean house.

LESSON

You cannot move forward if there are energies in your life that are holding you back.

IS YOUR SPIRIT READY?

———

Are you really ready to go to the next level of your life? Are you really ready to eliminate some "friendships" so that you can move forward in your life and get even closer to God? Is your spirit ready for this?

If you are committed to living a life where God lives in your heart, you must take responsibility for the relationships you enter into and maintain. You must not justify your behavior or the behavior of others. If you are really going to live a life you love, you have to commit to living your truth. You have to take the path less taken and stand up for what your spirit needs. When spirit touches your heart, soul, and mind, and directs you to eliminate some folks from your life, you need to listen and take action.

It's powerful to get to the point of eliminating negative energy from your life, but when you're really ready to go to the next level and have relationships that are built on a spiritual connection, then you'll get rid of the people you're just tolerating, the people you are just allowing to be in your world, the people who are not adding anything to your world, the people who say they mean well but never help you feel any better, the toxic people. You will let go and claim a better future. You will claim better relationships. You will raise your standards and expectations. And when you do that, you will receive more blessings than you can imagine. When you do that, you will experience peace and happiness. If you're ready, then make the necessary changes.

LESSON

When spirit touches your heart, soul, and mind, and directs you to eliminate some folks from your life, you need to listen and take action.

DO YOU LIKE SETTLING?

———

Do you like settling? Oh, of course you do. You do it every day that you wake up and go to a job you hate. You do it every time you hold back your truth and just tell someone what he or she wants to hear. You do it when you allow people to stay in your life even though they don't give you their best. You allow yourself to stay in situations that are not spiritually fulfilling, and you choose to keep doing the same things over and over again. You settle each and every day. The question is, Will you stop settling?

Are you ready to stop settling? At some point in our lives, we have to know that we deserve more than we are getting. We have to know that the wisdom God instilled in us is ready to come out. We just have to find the method of bringing out our glorious wisdom. We have to move beyond the ordinary and find the things that make us extraordinary. But life only changes for those who are willing to stop being stagnant. Life only changes when we stop settling in all areas of our lives. Life can and will change when we give and accept only the best.

We are not put here to settle. We are not placed here to tolerate people and jobs. We are here to go to the highest levels possible. And each day we must decide how much farther and harder we are going to push in order to get the life we deserve.

LESSON

If you choose to live a life of mediocrity, then you will always settle in some area of your life. It is those who push toward greatness who will expect, receive, and give only the best in everything they do.

WILL YOU CREATE GREATNESS?

———

For those pursuing a dream, getting prepared is almost like going to the Olympics. It takes forever just to qualify to be in the game. You prepare for years just to get a chance to be judged. And then someone says yes, you're good enough, you can go to the game. You're all excited, inspired, and feeling damn good. Somebody finally let you in. Somebody is finally giving you a chance to show what you're made of. But then the excitement subsides, and you realize that you're really at the beginning again. Yeah, someone's let you in the game, but now you have to win the thing.

And you know that with all those years of preparation, hoping, and dreaming, you didn't come to win the silver or the bronze. You came to win the GOLD. The gold is your goal and that's all you see. It's not the time to look at your competitors and see what they're dealing with. You can't look back and judge your future performance on players who got a chance last year. This is your time. So you have to focus and win. You're in the game. All you have to do is win. Just like the Olympics, though, there may be thousands of people who came to play— you're not focused on them, what they're capable of, or what they're thinking. The only thing to think about is how to go home with the gold.

The thing about goals is that they are a continuous process. Sometimes you're at the beginning and sometimes you're at the end and another goal is on the horizon. You just have to be prepared to push with all that you have. You have to be comfortable with beginning again and again. You may feel like you are constantly starting over, and you are. But you're always starting from a new position. A little more insight has been gained, a little more wisdom, knowledge, and confidence.

Most people will fail because they're too busy looking at the obstacles, being intimidated by the statistics and facts, and creating excuses. A chosen few will remain focused on the goal, push with all the energy God gave them, and they will create greatness.

LESSON

It is easier to plan for a dream than it is to walk in the path of the dream and endure the journey.

LEAVE A LEGACY

———

Imagine if our Rev. Dr. Martin Luther King Jr. thought about all the people who were against him, felt threatened by the constant attempts made on his life, felt as though he were fighting for something that would never change, imagine if he gave up.

Where would you be?

Imagine if the jail stints were just too much. Imagine him looking into the eyes of his innocent children, shutting the door, and just staying home. Imagine if he said, It's not worth it. Imagine if he said, We can't defeat this. Imagine if he said, I give up.

Where would you be?

Though he had so many trials and serious threats coming at him, Dr. Martin Luther King Jr. never gave up. He never backed down or away from his convictions and beliefs. And though the human side surely felt the pain of everything going on in his life, his spirit never stopped fighting for what was right.

He knew that although he loved his precious children dearly, he couldn't stop fighting because he was a parent. If anything, he had to fight even harder to make the world better for them. He knew that his fight was bigger than his fears or doubts. He knew that his hand, his life, his spirit was in the hands of, and being guided by, something far greater than evil and doubt. God guided his life and he knew this as his truth.

For every trial, he knew God was there. For every obstacle, he knew God was there. He knew his God was bigger than everything he would face. He knew there was no excuse that can be justified when God has given your spirit the duty to do something.

In your life what excuse do you have that is bigger than fire hoses turned against you, dogs being let loose after you, death threats against your family, time in jail? What excuse do you have that stops you from living a life you love?

Rev. Dr. Martin Luther King Jr. died in his thirties and left a legacy. What will you be leaving? What will your legacy be?

You cannot continue to let obstacles block you. You cannot continue to stay in relationships that stifle your spirit. You cannot use your children as the reason why you do not do something.

You cannot continue to thank and pray to God and never believe that he will make your dreams come true. How big is your God? How strong is your faith?

Make a commitment now to live a life you love, and have faith in the process. Know that God will see you through. Know that it is meant for you. Thank God for each and every thing you go through. Thank him with your heart, spirit, and soul, and watch the blessings come into your life.

Dr. Martin Luther King Jr. knew that he was fighting for a better life for Americans. He questioned whether he would get to see that day. But his focus and reason for fighting was that other individuals would get to see that day. His fight was bigger than his individual needs.

LESSON

Make your life stand for something. Leave a legacy.

GET INTO YOUR LIFE

At some point in our lives, we get sick and tired of living and loving beneath our potential. So when you feel as though you're stuck between a rock and a hard place, how do you begin to make the necessary changes for your life? The first thing is to commit to making a change. So many people waste their life, time, and energy wishing and hoping for change. Rarely do they step outside of their routine to make the necessary changes. It is so much easier for people to talk about change rather than make the changes. It is so much easier to dissect the life of another, and say what you would or would not do if you were that person. Life is so easily lived when you live it on the sidelines.

To rise higher, you're going to have to go deeper into yourself, and figure out what you really want. You have to realize that you are creating your life every day. Are you wasting your time watching others fulfill their dreams by watching TV all night? Are you up talking on the phone complaining about work or listening to gossip? It is in these moments of idleness that we allow our destiny to slip farther and farther away.

You must live this day as if it is your last. Don't put off things that can and should be done today. Don't hold back from saying I love you or showing you care. Make the extra effort to push your dreams into reality. Stop waiting for the future, the right time, and appreciate this moment. This moment is all you have. This is the moment you are promised. Use it to your full advantage.

The next step is to stop listening to the wrong folks. There isn't anyone who can see your destiny more clearly than you. There isn't anyone who knows just how badly you want to see your dream materialize. There isn't anyone who can fulfill your dream for you. You have to be willing to stop listening, and start doing what's right for you. Listening to gossips stunts your growth. Listening to naysayers affects your spirit. Stop infecting your spirit by listening to the wrong folks.

The final step is to do the work. You see, we can visualize, we can believe, and we can pray, and then we must work. God is within us for a reason. God is within your spirit to help you create your life. The goal is to stop listening to the negativity, obstacles, and excuses that the mind can bring and start listening to the spiritual voice that tells you, "You can do it. You can make it."

LESSON

If you are truly sick and tired of the way your life is flowing, change the direction. Change! Stop talking about it. Stop hoping for it and simply make the changes. Take the first step toward your destiny.

LOVE OR FEAR?

———

Life finds its course when you allow your spirit to guide you. Like a gentle wave, our spirit is meant to guide us away from problems, bad relationships, doubts, and insecurities, and toward love in all its glory.

When life has given you more than you can handle, it is because you have not released control. When you do not understand what will fulfill you, you have not let go. When life seems overwhelming and like too much to bear, you have not let go.

There is a point in your life when you will have to make a choice to be a conscious participant in your life. This means that you allow yourself to live in love. You move away from all fear and slowly embrace love until it covers your entire life.

Love is what we are here for. Love is what we are meant to experience. Yet so many times life has hardened and embittered us, until we do not love or trust ourselves. You have to move back to your center, your spirit, and love yourself again.

Choose to take control of your life. In taking control, you are letting go of the mundane things of life and allowing God to lead you. In taking control of your life, you define who comes into your life and who must go. In taking control, you determine where you are going to go. You decide how life is going to fulfill you. You decide what you are going to pour into this life so that the same can be returned to you.

Love will allow you to see, do, and experience many wonderful things. Fear will have you singing the "why me?" blues.

It's all a choice. Either live in love or live in fear. What do you really want?

LESSON

Love the life you live.

RELEASE YOURSELF

It amazes me that so many people have the ability to say "I'm blessed, God is good" and similar sayings, yet when they are faced with a tough situation they cannot let go and let God guide them. It is so easy to believe in the power of God during the good times. It is so easy to inspire and motivate someone else when you're in a good place. It is very easy to say that you are blessed when there is no drama or negativity in your life. But when things change, as they will in life, people tend to get anxious and they start worrying and focusing on their problem.

It is at the moment of turmoil that the difference between stating you believe in the power of God and trusting in the power of God is made known. How many people do you know who say they believe in God, but during a difficult time they say, "I don't know how I'm going to make it through this"? How many people do you know who can smile and say they are blessed, but when a little adversity hits, they look as if they have the weight of the world on their shoulders?

Believing in God is not meant to occur in just the good moments of your life. When you believe in the power of God, you know that no matter what happens to you today or tomorrow, God's got your back. When you know the power of God, you do not have to embrace your worries, fears, and struggles, because you know that God can only work when you have surrendered. An anxious spirit cannot receive blessings. If you continue to worry about a problem and keep it in your head, your spirit becomes blocked against receiving the help and guidance that you need.

You must surrender all. Don't just sing it. Don't just say it. Embrace the knowledge that God has got your back, and there is not a person in this world who can block your blessings except you.

Believing, trusting, and knowing the power of God is the cure for every trouble you have. Release yourself from focusing on your stress and problems. Release yourself from feeling alone. Release yourself from feeling that you are the only one with the solution. Release yourself from worrying. In order to receive the answer, in order to be blessed, you have got to let go.

You have to let your words match your actions. Even when you are in pain, you are still blessed. Even when you are experiencing stress and grief, God is still good. God doesn't change, but we need to change our perspective and stop rejoicing and being grateful just during the good times. In your lowest moment, you should still thank God, because you're about to be brought through some things. If God has chosen for you to experience some difficulty right now, thank him, and realize that you are going to go higher in your life if you keep the right perspective, if you keep an open spirit and heart, and if you learn from your life.

Our praises to God must be consistent and appreciative for every moment he gives us—good and bad. Even during your painful moments, you should still be able to pull on the source of God, and inspire another person, and say with a pure heart, "I am blessed and God is good."

LESSON

God has got your back, and there is not a person in this world who can block your blessings except you.

SHAKE OFF THE SLUGGISHNESS

Every day in America millions of people engage in lives of mediocrity. The accepted reality for 95 percent of the population is that life is a struggle, jobs are not to be enjoyed, everyone has debt, and no one likes what they do for a living. And if, by age thirty, you have not found some way to overcome this negative mentality, you become either one of the walking dead, who gives in to the day-to-day reality of their lives and gives up on their dreams, you become bitter that you never got your "chance" to make it, or you continue to wish for a better life and wait for the right opportunity to come along.

So how do we change the direction in which we are headed?

For a couple of weeks I was very prone to falling. I never literally hit the ground, but I kept losing my balance. The reason was because I was sick with the flu and so I wasn't as focused as normal. I had a lack of energy and felt as if I was just making it through the day. Do you ever feel like that?

I felt like the best I could do was get up and do some work and chores that needed to be done, and then I just wanted to sit down somewhere and not think about anything. Do you ever feel like that? I noticed that the longer the illness stayed with me and drained me, the more enticing television shows became. Have you noticed yourself being drawn to the television lately?

You see, those flu symptoms I endured are the same symptoms 95 percent of Americans deal with every day. They're drained, have just enough energy to go to work, deal with traffic, and make dinner. Then they don't want to think about or do anything else.

That day, as I hit my toe one more time and almost fell again, I got the message God was giving me. I wasn't focused on my blessings, because I was too busy looking at what was wrong and looking at the obstacles in front of me. I was giving power to my weak moments, and that's where we get stuck in life. Just because you're in a painful position, or struggling right now, does not mean that you have to always be that way.

Just because your finances may be low right now does not mean that you have to stay that way. Stop focusing on what's wrong and look at what's right. You still have the ability to break the mold and make it into the 5 percent who love their lives and are living their dreams. You still have a chance to change things.

You may have been knocked around by life. You may have felt like you were going to fall. But God has always been there with you and he's not going to let you fall without picking you up. Take the lessons of your painful moments, and use them as fuel to take you higher, and as wisdom so that you never have to return to this painful place.

We all need to shake off the sluggishness and get to work. We have a purpose to fulfill, dreams to make happen, and lives to love.

LESSON

There are times in your life when you will want to give up. You cannot fall victim to your life. Failure is not an option.

THIS TOO SHALL PASS

Throughout every major experience I've had in life (from dealing with being molested, to relationship breakups, to becoming a single mother), I always knew that whatever pain I was dealing with in the moment was only for the moment. I would not give anything or anyone complete power over me. I knew in my heart, "this too shall pass."

It is an underlying strength that I am very aware of. It has gotten me out of painful situations and terrible moments. It has helped me to see that though I may have made emotional decisions, I still had the power to change my life. I had what was necessary to make major life changes. I had true faith.

So many of us talk of faith. So many of us want faith. Faith to me is knowing, without a doubt, that God will see me through and get me to where I am destined to be. I know that there is not a human in this world who can stop that process or progress. What is meant for me will be. There are no alternatives.

God has all of our lives mapped out. And though it can feel like we've gotten caught up, off track, and there is no way back, there is always a way. When you can get on your knees with a full and humble heart and say, "God, please help me. Help me get through," he will answer you.

Any *true* cry to God will get answered. I have been there and lived the experience. God will not only lift you up, he will release you into a world you could not have imagined.

Allow God to hear your cry. Allow God to take all your fears, doubts, worries, and insecurities away. Allow God to take the pain of whatever happened to you in your childhood and adulthood away. Allow God to be the strength and guide in your life. Then life will change for you.

You will see and know that no problem is insurmountable. No person can take away God from you. And if they cannot take away the God that exists within you, then they can never take away who you are.

It hurts my spirit to see someone hold on to his or her painful past. It's like an emotional anchor that they don't know how to let go of. Some people have been holding on to their pain for so long they're no longer aware of how long its been building up within them.

You have to release yourself so that you can move on. If there is at least one area in your life where you are settling or holding on to painful moments, you will block your full blessings in other areas. You will not feel the peace of love and happiness for yourself. If you are still holding on to any anger, you cannot experience true love. If you are still holding on to any pain, you cannot experience true joy. If you do not know that God will handle pain for you, then you are not experiencing true spiritual happiness.

At this moment, make a decision to be conscious of your choices. Release yourself from all pain. Remove yourself from a painful past. Empower yourself by reclaiming your essence. Unleash your spirit into the world and you will be a force to be reckoned with. For now, forever, and always, God has your back and no one can take that away from you.

"This too shall pass." You will live a life you love!

LESSON

No person can take God away from you. And if they cannot take away the God that exists within you, then they can never take away who you are. They can never take your soul and spirit unless you give it away.

DO YOU SUFFER FROM THIS?

———

You have to be careful of becoming a victim of the complex syndrome that paralyzes its victims. It gives them heart palpitations, and many suffer from anxiety, migraines, and lack of energy. The syndrome is called—What If. You may have a dream and a plan to change your life, but What If . . . You know you deserve better from a relationship, but What If . . . You know God has to have better things in store for you, but What If . . . You know you have talent, but What If . . . You know you're being treated poorly, but What If . . .

You can become so overwhelmed by the What If's that you will literally suffer from analysis paralysis. You will analyze the situation so intently that you become stuck in your situation. Suddenly the obstacles seem to loom over you. Life feels difficult and as though it is suffocating you. You would change your life, but What If . . .

The key to delivering yourself from this syndrome is to answer positively. What if God wants more for me and I'm just holding myself back? What if once I get going, life just gets better and better? What if it's my time to shine? What if I need to make these moments count?

What if this was your time to step out on faith, but you kept holding yourself back because you're afraid of moving forward? What if you are the only one holding yourself back from greatness? You know what? You are the only one who can hold you back from living a life you love. You are the only one who can change your life. You are the one who has to stop giving yourself excuses and start getting over the obstacles.

LESSON

The biggest obstacles we face are the ones that dwell in our minds.

BE CAREFUL WHO YOU HANG AROUND

When I was young my father would always tell me, "Be careful who you hang around, it will determine where you go in life." At the time, I thought he was talking Chinese, especially since I was only in the fourth grade. But as I look at things in life now, I realize those words were golden.

Whom we choose to hang around can directly affect where we go in life. Whom we choose as lovers and friends affects our mindset and energy. Before making a decision to call someone a friend, make sure you know this person. See if they are there in your good and bad times.

I had a friend from high school who was there through the terrible times of my relationship. She shared every tear with me and gave me cards and words of encouragement. The day my publisher called to say I would be featured in their advertising campaign, I called her excitedly. She said she could not be happy for me. She felt as though I had taken away a dream from her. It had always been her secret wish to write.

Though I felt overwhelmed, I thanked her for her honesty. Then I simply thought if you cannot handle this, then you cannot handle my future, because I am just getting started. And I haven't talked to her since.

You see, there are some people who are meant to stay in our lives for a while. There are some who are only meant to share a lesson and help us learn something about ourselves. Then there are some people who will share this life journey with us. At the worst possible moment, you will find out who is your friend and who is not. Thank God for showing you, and make a decision then to get all negative energy out of your life.

You have every right to choose who comes into your life. This is your choice, your decision, and your life. If you want it to be fulfilling and prosperous, then bring in people who can enhance your life.

LESSON

At the worst possible moment, you will find out who is your friend and who is not. Thank God for showing you, then make a decision to get all negative energy out of your life.

WE CHOOSE OUR EXPERIENCES

I remember a few years ago I loved a man so deeply that I nearly lost my mind. In my world of today, he wouldn't be given a second thought. But oh, back then. Back then. Back then. I LOVED him. You would've thought the sun rose and set based on him. You would've thought that time stopped until he decided what to do. Okay, maybe it wasn't that deep. But you get my point. I loved this man. I was choosing to love him deeply and unconditionally. I wanted to experience love so much that I disregarded the "getting to know each other" phase and jumped right into "I'm in love."

We make so many of our foolish choices based on how we feel. If we took the time to be rational rather than emotional, there would be far less drama, and probably less children, in the world. The number of children born because of casual sex is staggering. The number of people who enter into relationships without taking the time to get to know each other is mind-blowing. So many of us continue to live ridiculous lives because we do not realize the power of choice. We do not realize how powerful our minds are.

Instead, we live our whole life based on how we feel. Or how someone else will feel about what we do. It's all just ridiculous.

Let me tell you about this man I loved so much. If I had taken a few more days, weeks, or months to just slow down and get to know him, I would've seen past the façade and into the interior. If I had not been so absorbed in the great energy we had, I would have been able to see him in his element. When times are rough, how will this person be then? When times are good, how will he be then? When people are praising me and disregarding him, how will he be then?

How will someone fit into your life? That's the question that needs to be asked. Do they bring joy? Do they bring wisdom? Do they bring the pain of their experiences or the lessons they have received?

Before you set yourself on a path of love, find out if you like someone. Find out if they deserve to be in your life. Did I say deserve? Sure did. Do they deserve to be in your life? Can the God in you see the God in them?

Though God is manifest in everyone, there are some folks who haven't found him yet. They're not living in glory. They're not living in joy. They are merely existing and surviving. And if you allow them, they will waste their time and yours.

There are people who enter our lives to teach us a lesson. But there are also people we hold on to for too long. We give them power over our lives because we *choose* to live through the heart and not the spirit and mind. We choose to ignore what is essential to our spirit.

We choose everything we experience. We choose how long to deal with a situation. We choose what to tolerate and what to endure. We choose our life.

If we took a moment to really accept that into our spirit—we choose our life—there would be a whole lot of changes going on right now. People would be doing what they love, and loving who they really wanted to love. People would choose to experience love and joy, rather than struggle and pain. People would choose happiness, rather than joining in pity parties. People would choose to live their life based on the needs of their spirit, and do what's right for their well-being. Indeed, people would be a bit more selfish because they would choose their happiness first.

Can selfishness help change the course of our lives? The answer is, in order to give happiness, you must be happy. In order to give love, you must be loving. In order to trust, you must be willing to trust and be trustworthy. You must be the very thing that you want. So yes, you must be selfish in your pursuit to fulfill your passion. You must be selfish in your quest to be happy. You must be selfish in your desire to live drama-free. You must be willing to fight for your happiness, and realize your power; then you will go to another level in your life.

LESSON

Life is about choice. We are all given a choice every day to choose love or fear, happiness or pain, wealth or poverty.

FEAR WILL DO WHATEVER YOU ALLOW IT TO DO

It sits in your mouth and blocks your ability to speak. It sits in your heart and blocks your ability to dream. It gets in your spirit and creates obstacles for you. It gets in your mind and makes you question yourself. It makes you think that you are unable and unworthy.

Fear will do whatever you allow it to do.

There is healthy fear and there is negative fear. Healthy fear is when you are still afraid yet you continue to step out on faith, walk toward your dreams, believe in a better life, and just make things happen regardless of what your circumstances may say. You move forward in spite of whatever experiences you are going through now, because you know your final outcome is better than where you are now. You have decided to allow fear to be your motivation rather than your limitation.

Our fear allows us to remain humble while we continue to proceed toward our best life. When we are humble, God is able to enter our heart, spirit, and mind. When God has entered us, there is no fear or negativity that can be formed to defeat us. Keep moving forward. Embrace the fear. Walk with the fear. Just don't stop moving. Don't stop believing. Be courageous. Be powerful. Be consistent. Be humble.

LESSON

Courage is the ability to feel fear in your heart and still keep moving.

THERE ARE ANGELS
SURROUNDING YOU

———

In your life, every day, if you are aware, you can encounter angels.

An angel or teacher is someone who enters our life at just the right moment with the needed words, support, push, or nudge.

An angel is there to push us farther along our path. An angel will guide us, when we are willing to listen.

When I think of it, it's almost like a small whisper. Your angel will speak to you through your subconscious. Then she will speak to you through others. Finally, she will work on the behalf of God to make your life change so much that you have to make a change.

When people tell you from their heart what they see for you, listen. When more than one person explains their pain and shows you a way out, listen. When someone says please don't go the route I went, listen.

Most people will try to help you do what's right for you. If you trust in God, then you must trust in the goodness of spirit that exists within others. God uses that spirit to guide you to your higher truth, your best life.

But are you capable of listening? Do you have the strength to walk out on faith with just the fact that God has your back?

Do you believe in yourself enough to know that since God

gave you the dream, all you have to do is begin the steps toward achieving it and it will begin to unfold?

Do you listen to God? Or do you simply keep talking to him, praying, pleading, begging, but never once being quiet and just listening?

Do you have it in you to listen to God when he tells you to get up out of the hell of life you're living and walk? Just walk, and he will lead you. Can you do that?

Most people can't. Most people won't. They don't believe in themselves. They don't have enough faith, strength, or courage. They would rather hold on to excuses than attempt to overcome the obstacles. They would rather justify the pain than come out and say this is enough. They would rather find the few moments of good in their life than say I deserve more than this. God wants better for me than this.

Most people don't have what it takes to step out, hold God's hands, and believe that they will achieve.

Do you believe in angels? Do you believe in God? Do you believe in dreaming or do you believe in achieving?

Angels are everywhere. When they talk, you need to listen. When you hear the same things over and over again about your life, look at the pattern and make a change.

Listen to your life. It will show you who you are and where you are headed. Then just know without a doubt, that no matter where you are in life, you can change the results. You can change your life.

You just have to want it, believe it, know it, claim it, focus on it, thank God for it, and see it happening in your life.

Begin the journey to a better life. Make that much-needed change in your life. Show God that you believe in his power, and he will bless you more than you can imagine.

LESSON

Listen to your life. It will show you who you are and where you are headed.

SELFISHNESS CAN BE A BLESSING

When I was younger, I was very selfish. I did not do anything I didn't want to do. I didn't go out of my way to do anything for anyone. I looked at my best interests first and then did for others (if I had to). My focus was on what I wanted. My family called me manipulative. Boyfriends called me spoiled. My best friends were just like me, we called it being strong.

I received my humbling moment when I was only nineteen. I felt God come into my heart. I knew then that I was being prepared for something. I just didn't know what. But at that moment I felt peace and the "lightness" of spirituality. Then I began the worst years of my life.

Between the ages of twenty and twenty-five I learned so much about myself. I learned what I was capable of and how much pain I could withstand. I learned the blessings of true friendship. I learned that family could sometimes be your worst enemy. I learned how to genuinely say "thank you." I learned to appreciate the actions and attention of others. I thank everyone and God for every little thing now.

I appreciate my life. I appreciate my blessings. I appreciate those challenging years because God allowed me to change and let my spirit take over me. I became a woman who can understand and empathize. I became capable of inspiring others in a positive way.

I talked with my mother recently. I was telling her how selfish a friend in my life was being. My mother replied, "More selfish than you." I could only laugh and leave that comment alone.

It used to annoy and hurt me that my family couldn't see that I was no longer that selfish teenage girl. Then it hit me. They still have me linked with selfishness, but what is so bad about that selfishness now?

Being selfish, as a youth, has allowed me to never be taken advantage of in a relationship. It has allowed me to have strength and confidence in business situations. It has allowed me to have great respect and assurance for myself. It has allowed me to never give so much that I give my power or myself away. I have never had the inability to say no. I have always had the power to say no.

Many women do not have the ability to say no to friends and family. At the age of forty-something is when most women finally have the ability to turn off the need-to-please and focus on them.

You know what, I've never had that problem. I'm not waiting until I'm forty to tell someone how I feel. I know my limitations, and that is a blessing. I know just how much I am capable of, and that is a blessing. I know when my spirit, time, energy, and/or love are being misused on someone, and that is a blessing.

I know that if I do not take care of me, then I will not be able to take care of anyone else. I know that if I do not love myself more than anyone else, then I will never be able to give pure love. I know that the world must revolve around me in order for me to see my significance and purpose in life. I know that being selfish, as a youth, has allowed me to be a powerful woman now. So now I thank God for that quality too.

Appreciate all your strengths and blessings. If someone is trying to hold you back based on your past, release him or her from your thoughts. Never allow anyone to hold you back in any way. This is your life to claim, control, enjoy, and love! It's all about you. See the beauty in who you are, and appreciate every quality you have. Everything you are is a gift from God. Don't hide your spirit.

LESSON

Never allow anyone to hold you back in any way

IT ALL BEGINS WITH LISTENING

———

There is a voice that exists within us that is meant to serve as a guide. So many people encounter difficulty and frustration because they did not heed the requests of that little voice. How many times have you asked yourself a question about your life and then ignored the answer? It wasn't that you thought the answer was wrong. In fact, you knew that was the decision you should make. You simply chose not to listen.

We have to stop feeling so overwhelmed by life. We need to realize that we do have the ability to gain control over our life. It all begins with listening. Listen to your spirit as it tells you what is right for you through that inner voice. Listen to the lessons of your life. Observe your life and make conscious choices.

You are in control of your life. You can and will have power over your life once you begin to listen. My life goes so much better, so much easier, when I listen to that little voice. There have been times when the voice has said remember to bring this or that with you, and I want to question that statement, but I have learned to listen. And then, "uncoincidentally," I need exactly what that little voice told me to bring with me.

To empower yourself, you must know that you are responsible for your life. You are responsible for the choices you make. But you are never alone in life. You are always just a question away from getting the answers you need. You just have to commit to following the advice. You just have to know that God talks to you through that voice. And in order to feel empowered, confident, and wise, you must listen to that voice.

There is power in listening.

LESSON

The answers lie within; all you have to do is ask.

PRAY HARD

———

Remember the last time you were in so much pain that you doubled over, dropped to your knees, and just began praying? The pain was so intense that all you could say was, "God please take this away. God please help me." And this became your mantra. You repeated it and repeated it, hoping that the pain would subside. You were praying hard to be released from the pain. You believed wholeheartedly that only God could take away this pain. There was no drug to cure this pain. In that moment, it was only you and God. Remember how hard you prayed?

Then the pain started to subside. It wasn't as unbearable. And you cried and swayed and thanked God. Every fiber of your being was grateful and appreciative of God's blessing. You were in the middle of being healed and you knew it. You could feel it. You acknowledged his greatness and the pain subsided some more.

Then you became fully healed. You were able to get up and stand on your feet. You slowly became strong again, and as the pain subsided, the appreciation you had for God subsided too. You weren't praying as hard. You weren't saying thank you to God for every little thing anymore. You started to take your health and blessings for granted.

God is not only there for us in our down and painful moments, he is there for us in our joyful and peaceful moments as well. Prayers during our joy and our pain need to be filled with the same intensity. Just as you can pray hard and thank God so much for being healed, you can pray hard and thank God for being blessed, for being able to laugh, for not being in pain.

LESSON

Appreciate your life; it's God's gift to you.

YOU GET WHAT YOU EXPECT

———

So many people live limited lives. They continue to make choices that help them to remain stagnant. They make choices that block their growth and productivity. So many people get caught up in their day-to-day world and lose sight of the things they really want. For those who do have a dream, you have to finally get sick and tired of a life in which your dreams are unfulfilled. You have to get tired of where you are now. You have to be sick of where you're headed. You have to realize that every day is an opportunity to create a better future. So commit to your happiness.

Commit to your life. Make choices that empower and change your world. One of my lessons in life has been around relationships. I realize that I have to admire and be in awe of the man in my life. I want to be inspired. I want a man who has strength.

I remember doing an evaluation of my life and looking at the people in it. I remarked at the time that I had yet to meet a man. I had yet to meet a strong man. I had to realize that in many ways, I was expecting them to be weak. I was expecting to be the more ambitious one. I was expecting to be the one who makes things happen. So I got what I expected. I would get men who suddenly realized, after being around me, that they needed to get themselves together. I would get men who realized that they were not where they wanted to be in life. I would get men with cloudy dreams or no vision. I would get men living without a purpose. And you know what? I realized that I was creating this world. I was getting exactly what I believed they were capable of giving.

So I committed to raising my expectations. I came to trust God. I had to believe that if I have God in my life, then there are single men with God in their life as well. I stopped settling in my endeavors. For all my adult life, I had been meeting the same man; different face, different body, but the same man. Finally, I said good-bye to him. I released myself from meeting these men. I pushed myself to the next level. I believe that as I move to the higher levels, there will be a relationship that is able to encompass all that I am, and all that I have to offer. I know that whatever door I am willing to go through, my expectations will be surpassed. I know that if God gives you the vision, the hope, the clarity, and the blessing of wanting more, you will be rewarded. It's just a matter of stepping up.

As I claimed the right to go to higher levels and came to believe that there were strong men in the world, my focus changed. My beliefs changed. My expectations changed. And then, the strong men appeared.

Powerful, inspirational, awesome men, and I thank them for their friendship. I thank them for being a blessing in my life. And I thank God that I knew when to let go of negative thoughts. Take yourself to the next level and say good-bye to debilitating thoughts. Say good-bye to relationships that are holding you back. Claim your life. Claim your happiness. Create your life while you still have the chance.

Here are the good-byes I made that day:

Good-bye, weak man

Good-bye, man with no vision

Good-bye, man with no purpose

Good-bye, man with no power

Good-bye, man of excuses

Good-bye, man who lives in the past

Good-bye, man with no ambition

Good-bye, man who doesn't know God

Good-bye, man who lives with fear

Good-bye, insecure man

Good-bye, man who tries to bring me down

Good-bye, man who tries to make me question myself

Good-bye, man who tries to drain my power

Good-bye, man who speaks negative thoughts

Good-bye, man without spirit

Good-bye, man without love

Good-bye, good-bye, good-bye

LESSON

Commit to your happiness.

MAYBE YOU'RE NOT SUFFERING ENOUGH

People have a greater ability to make excuses than to make decisions. It is easier to negate responsibility and avoid confrontation. It is easier to look at an obstacle than to remain focused on the goal. It is more natural for most people to complain about their life than it is for them to make a change.

A minister told a story of a woman coming to him and complaining. It seemed as if she were barely pausing to take a breath. She told the minister that nothing was going right in her life. She was frustrated with her job and her relationship. She just didn't know what to do. All she could say was, "I'm suffering."

The minister, who was very tired after just giving the sermon, looked at her and replied, "You're not suffering enough."

To say the woman was devastated is an understatement. Her mouth dropped and she stared at him as if he were an alien. The minister noticed her reaction, but when asked how he could say such a thing, he replied again, "You're not suffering enough."

Realizing that he didn't want the woman to pass out, he said, "Imagine you picked up a very hot pot with your bare hands. Do you hold on to it and say it's not that hot, I can hold it? Do you keep holding it so that you can see how much pain you can withstand? No, if the pot were too hot you would put it down immediately. But you are allowing your problems to be like that pot. You're trying to be strong by holding on to something that you shouldn't be holding on to anyway. If you had suffered enough, you would let all these problems go now."

We all tend to be that woman at times in our lives. We hold on to people and situations that are detrimental to our well-being. We justify things. We make excuses. We limit ourselves from living a life of happiness because we are afraid to make changes. We are afraid to live a life we love.

There are many people who don't want to love life. They like being a part of the majority that struggles. They enjoy having "friendships" that allow them to remain stagnant. They enjoy having jobs that have nothing to do with their purpose or the power of their spirit. They enjoy having a spouse or lover that they cannot stand or relate to. Oh yes, they enjoy it. If they didn't enjoy these painful things, they would not tolerate them.

You would never be tempted to look back on a past that is painful and paint it as pretty. You wouldn't try to find the few good memories in a relationship that, overall, just took you to levels you never thought you would go to. You wouldn't be in pain if you really wanted to love life. You would be free.

Assume that God wants to give you everything you *need*. Assume that there are angels waiting to guide you toward your best life. Believe that God is willing to give you the love and life you have only dreamed about. Understand that God has a bigger dream for you than you have for yourself.

Now, here's the test. In front of you is a life you will love and cherish, behind you is the painful past of unfulfilling jobs and relationships. Imagine on this day, that God says to you—eliminate all the negativity in your life, walk toward me, and I will give you your soul's desire. But you cannot look back. You cannot glorify that which is not meant to be glorified.

Can you eliminate the negative elements in your life and walk with God toward a life you love?

LESSON

We limit ourselves from living a life of happiness because we are afraid to make changes.

JUST A CHILD

———

A mother came into her home and saw that her child had made a mess. She immediately began to yell and scream that he had made her house a mess and had just been sitting around wasting time. When he began to do what she asked, she yelled for him to get out of her way. She didn't want to see him. She began to clean the mess herself and anger enveloped her heart.

She walked past the child's room in disgust as he sat with his head down. She called his name and he looked up. She had to take a step back in awe. She didn't know if it was the lighting behind him but somehow there was a glow. An aura was surrounding her young child. And then a voice said, "I will not tell you in what shape I will come, when I will come, or how I will come. All I ask is that you love me as I love you. Love one another as I love you. I don't love you just in your good moments. I love you and treat you with love all the moments of your life."

The woman began to cry. The light shifted on the boy's face and she could see the face of her young child. He was only a child. He didn't understand that her day had been long and she was frustrated about her job. He had no idea she was making just enough to pay the bills. He was simply a child who had been playing and was not concerned about the upkeep of the house. So when his mother came into the house with anger he ingested her anger into his soul. He took it personally and felt as though she didn't love him.

We cannot do this to our children. We cannot do this to one another. When you say you love God, you must see God within others and treat them with love. No matter what we do in life, God is always there. We are never greeted with an angry or unforgiving spirit. No matter what we do, God continues to welcome us, to love us, and to cherish us. We must realize, as parents, that we are the same source. Our children turn to us for the loving support their spirit needs, just as we turn to God.

LESSON

Treat others the same way you would want God to treat you—with love!

HE WHO DELIBERATES

———

They say that if you hear something over and over again, it will become ingrained in your mind and incorporated into your spirit. As I looked at yet another e-mail with inspirational and motivational information, I had to shake my head and wonder. If we are all passing around this positive energy and sharing Bible verses with one another, why aren't we living our true purpose?

I mean, if we really believe what we are reading, what is taking us so long to GET IT? What is taking us so long to live lives we love? There's got to be a point in life when you stop just listening to the great sermons, stop just reading the inspirational messages, stop just getting pumped up from motivational messages, and actually start doing something.

What will it take? It can't be more inspirational messages. It can't be another good word from the preacher or a good song.

In the end, it's going to take a commitment from you. One of my favorite quotes is by Abraham Lincoln. Lincoln said, "Things may come to those who wait, but only the things left by those who hustle." So the question to ask is—Are you hustling? Or are you being complacent? Or do you just like making excuses?

You see, if your back was to the wall and you just had to make some changes, you would make them now. If a doctor told you that you only had six months to live, you would LIVE more in those six months than you have in your entire life. If you lost your source of income today, you would be on the phone tomorrow putting your talents to work. So why not now? Why not hustle now? Why not push for the life you really want now?

It is deceptively easy to get lost in your life. It is very easy to get caught up in the whirlwind of working and paying bills. It is easy to believe that everyone must work for money instead of money working for you. It is easy to believe that everyone has a job and is Just Over Broke, so why would you be any different? It is easy to believe the negative things, because if you believed for one second that you deserved the positive things—more money, freedom, time to live your life—your spirit would become so uncomfortable, you would be so unsettled, that you would be forced to make a change.

And so, many of us sit in lives we do not like, in cubicles that stunt our growth, because it is easier to talk about a dream than it is to get up and live the dream. It is easier to commiserate with someone about money problems than it is to create another source of income (or so we are led to believe).

It's time to take the shackles off our mind. We're creating our own prisons and making them tolerable because we know people who dream like we do, because people send inspirational messages, because the Bible verse touched our heart. While it helps us in some ways, it is not enough to have people understand the struggle toward a dream. It is not enough to have someone send you a message that touches your heart. What we all really need is people who are not just spreading a good message, but being the message.

We have to move forward in our lives. We have to believe

that freedom is just up the road and we have to begin walking toward it.

LESSON

Make a promise to yourself today:

I promise to stop making excuses for my life.

I promise not to settle in any area of my life.

I promise to listen to the needs of my spirit and the words of God.

I promise to live a life of purpose and fulfillment.

I promise to live a life of happiness and love.

I promise to stay focused.

I promise to be persistent in the pursuit of my dreams.

I promise to expand my vision and cast away my fears and doubts.

I promise to push fear aside when my spirit says it is time to step out on faith.

I promise to stop crying over the pain and start seeing the lesson and the blessing.

I promise to thank God for every moment.

I promise to live my life divinely and allow myself to live abundantly.

I promise myself these things because I deserve it and am entitled to it.

Remember this:

He who deliberates fully before taking a step, will spend his entire life on one leg.

—Chinese proverb

WHAT ARE YOUR INTENTIONS?

———

On the journey to becoming a better person, a spiritual person, there are choices and decisions to be made. If we are not truly listening to God and are tuning out our spirit, then life choices become difficult. We add the element of confusion into our lives when we tune out our spirit and focus on the "reality" of the world. We make life a struggle when we choose to "exist" rather than surpass our expectations and truly LIVE.

We must realize that we make choices every day in our lives. A choice either moves you forward or backward. It either pushes you toward love or toward fear. Your choices help to create the existence you are experiencing now. So what is the intention behind your choices?

My friend called the other day with a lot on her mind. She was stressed about marriage, love, and relationships. She wondered if love, in its purest form, ever exists. She was talking about her friends who are getting married. Friends who are choosing to get married even though they are in painful, unfulfilling, and abusive relationships.

My friend wondered if she was expecting too much from her relationships. She questioned whether her idea of love was more fantasy than reality.

As I pointed out to her, she wasn't in a relationship. She was dating someone off and on that she felt comfortable with. He didn't treat her well. She didn't treat him well. However, they call it love because some years have gone by. They call it love because they had grown up together. They were misusing the word and she was looking for someone to tell her to "settle" for what she had now.

Love is so many things. It is not painful, doubtful, or boastful. It does not bring you down. It does not make you question who you are and what you are capable of. It does not make you feel as though you have to "lower" your standards in order to be a part of something.

We make a choice to call things love rather than what they truly are. We have misconceptions. We base our relationships on the relationships of our friends and family. We base our expectations on what others around us have received. We say we love someone, then never give him or her the love their spirit deserves. We misuse the word *love*. We focus on the wrong things.

It frustrates me when so many people focus on marriage rather than the relationship. Choose what you want from your life. Know what you will and will not accept. Know in your heart and soul that the relationship you have now is not going to change when you say "I do."

When you love someone, you accept him or her the way they are right now. Love is not about hoping for change in someone. It is accepting someone's spirit.

So before you limit love to what others believe and are giving or receiving, look at God as love. Before you say a word, ask yourself, what would love (God) do? Then do it. Love has no limitations or boundaries. God in no way wants you to limit your spirit or blessings.

Open up to the true possibility of love. Define yourself by God's expectations of and for you, not by what others think. You deserve so much more. Live an authentic life in which love is expressed through your being into everything you do.

When you act through love, live in love, and work for love's sake, you will receive rewards.

Just as with the best business, the best life is one that truly helps another person.

LESSON

Love never has and never will make you become less than you are intended to become.

TRUE LOVE

———

In any minute you can be more
do more
give more
but the essence of finding it
of releasing it
is taking time to be you
for you
allow your spirit time to heal
and breathe
and see the world
without the constant turmoil
of new relationships and pain
allow your spirit to heal
and take you to a new level
open yourself up to loving yourself
and then
you will be able to experience
what true love is
how joy really feels

you will know
what it is like to feel God
within you
you will only feel your power
once you have taken the time
to get to know
and love yourself
embrace the divine within

Love yourself

WHAT WILL YOU FIGHT FOR?

———

Have you ever watched a loved one die? Have you been there through all the stages?

Imagine when they first get diagnosed with a life-threatening illness. At this point, you're doing everything you can to fight for their life with them. You're doing research and attending workshops. You're seeking advice from every doctor possible. You're fighting as if your life is on the line.

Then they get progressively worse. They are losing the battle. You watch in desperation unsure of what to do. You want to fight for them and be their strength and hope. You want to eradicate this disease from their body. You wish for more chances and more time to be with them.

You realize that they're dying painfully. You can see the hope fading from their eyes only to be replaced by pools of despair. You realize they're no longer fighting for their life. They want to give up so badly. They realize they are losing this battle and they are slowly allowing everything to subside. Their strength and vitality is no longer present.

You know you can no longer fight if they're not fighting. You simply watch as they begin to fade away. The tears no longer come, just the hope that they pass peacefully.

Now just imagine that dying person was actually your community. Where are you in the fight to save the community? Are you still fighting or just watching? Do you still have hope or faith? Do you feel it's time to give up?

Do you feel protected because you're not immediately connected to the problem? Are you aware that as long as you are here on this earth, you are connected to each and every person? Do you realize that you are here for a reason and purpose much larger than your individual needs? Do you know that your strength is needed? Do you know that without you, people will begin to fade away? Our community may just die that slow death. All the while you thought it had nothing to do with you. It's a matter of overcoming that "just existing/surviving" mentality and becoming a force to reckon with.

Make a commitment to yourself and to God to fight for what is right for the spirits on this earth. Push yourself beyond mental limits. Live life through your spirit. It is the most powerful thing you possess.

Never give up!

LESSON

We can all change the world; it's the only way true change is made—one person at a time.

LIFE IS A CHOICE

Imagine, if you will, living a life where every day you are doing what you hate. In fact, you dread getting up in the morning to begin a life of torture. You are living a life that is filled with mundane activities and unfulfilling chores.

Who chose this punishment for you? How did your life become a hell of just getting by, just surviving, just paying the bills? So many people continue at jobs they hate, and relationships that are frustrating, because they feel obligated. People feel trapped by their life and life choices.

As they go through the battle of their life, they feel the weight of their problems constantly. Life becomes overwhelming and frustrating. So many people believe that this is what life is about, surviving and maintaining yet never achieving happiness.

We have the power to eliminate unhappiness in our life. We can make a choice to live a life we love. We can choose whom we allow into our life. We do have the power and the God-given gifts to create a life we love.

We must trust our abilities and ourselves. Do not think that you are trapped in a life of misery. Instead, envision the way you want life to be. Focus on the good qualities you possess. Appreciate your talents and blessings. Take your focus off the problems and center on the solutions.

The answers to making your life better are all within. Listen to God. Trust God and you will get through any pain you are experiencing. A painful moment is just a stepping-stone in your life. You are on your way to greatness. You simply must commit to living a better life and creating the circumstances to make your dreams reality.

Our faith is our endurance. Our hope is the catalyst. Our spirit is our strength. Our belief is the vision shaper. Our soul is the guide. Just believe in yourself and focus on achieving your dreams.

LESSON

Commit to living a better life, and create the circumstances to make your dreams reality.

BEING TESTED IS A BLESSING

When you get to a point in life where you feel as though you are being pulled in many directions—too many directions—realize that it is at this moment that your spirit is being called upon.

When you have gotten to a point where you feel as though you cannot handle another bit of stress, worry, anxiety, or pain, realize that you are being chosen.

God loves you so much that he is giving your spirit the chance to know him better. Every time you call on God, you gain the opportunity to grow closer to him.

I want you to drop all the beliefs you have for a second and focus. Focus on the thought that God is love. You are created in his image; therefore, you are love manifest. You are love.

For you to truly learn how to express love and live in love, you have to go through some things. You have to come to a point where you truly know what love is, what it feels like. In essence, through the painful moments, you will come to know who you are and who your true friends are. You will explore love in its purest form—the moment when it is tested.

You are blessed to experience life and learn from it. You are blessed if God has chosen you to learn a lesson from him. He is choosing to bring you back into his fold. He is choosing to show you what love is.

LESSON

Every time you call on God, you gain the opportunity to grow closer to him.

GIVE WHAT YOU WANT

I have met many people and know many people who call themselves nice. The reality, though, is that many people are not as nice as they could or should be. They do not want to give what is not given to them. They do not want to give more than was given to them. They are basing their reactions, actions, and relationships on what was given to them.

This is such an injustice to your spirit and growth. You must always seek to give the love that was not given. Give the relationship that was not expected. Give the friendship you would always cherish. Give what you want, do not expect it in return, and you will be blessed.

Blessings do not come through self-definition; they come through the actions of your spirit, the strength of your character, the reliance of your being.

So many times we want to read the words of God, acknowledge the words of God, but rarely ever do we ACT on the words of God. Do unto others as you would want done to you. No other interpretation. Not do as was done to you.

To me spirituality is not just a journey, it is a destination you reach every day. Every day God will place situations into your life to see how you will act.

Will you act as one who has love in his or her heart? Or will you react out of anger, greed, suspicion, mistrust, or lack of communication? If it is anything other than love, it is not spirituality. For spirituality is based in love.

Spirituality is not only about becoming a person of love. It is about giving pure love, living in love, and treating others with love.

LESSON

Give what you want, do not expect it in return, and you will be blessed.

YOU HAVE TO GO THROUGH IT FIRST

———

The theme occurring in my life right now is, to whom much is given, much is expected. And if you intend to teach others through the lessons you have learned, then you will endure lessons continuously so that you may have something to share.

I believe God has an amazing sense of humor. He also has an excellent teaching pattern. All my life I have wanted to help others. But I was very judgmental. I could not understand how people could create lives of misery. I could not understand why people would choose to live a life of unhappiness.

I had no understanding that people needed to grow at their own pace. I was judging people on whether they had done what *I* thought they should have done. Or what I believed I would have done in that situation. Not by what they were capable of or what they wanted for themselves.

It has been shown to me that if you want to teach something, you have to go through it first. You have to experience some things in order to truly teach and reach others.

So rather than just sending an epiphany, God allowed me to experience the moments of doubt, insecurity, fear, pain, and a bad relationship. He showed me why people make certain choices in their lives. He showed me that things are not always what they seem.

God changed my perspective from "I can tell you" to "I

can show you" how to get through. So although painful, I can explain how I changed my life. I can share how I overcame being molested. I can share how I dealt with a business loss. I can share how I felt when my father called me all sorts of names. I can share with you how it felt to have my self-esteem lowered.

To be given a gift is a reward, to utilize it is a blessing. So no matter how painful life is at any moment, no matter what difficulty you are going through, if you can look at it through your divine spirit, you can appreciate it and grow from it.

It is God's wish to have you be more than you can imagine. It is his wish that you share some of that love he has for you with others. It is his wish that you appreciate everything he gives you, no matter how small or large.

It may not always feel like it, but if you are open to the lessons, you will always be pushed toward becoming a better person.

Growth never comes the way we expect it. Anyone can be a teacher; you just have to be open to the lesson. And if you truly believe and want spiritual growth, then you have to accept and incorporate the lessons you learn into your life. This allows you to control your destiny and your spiritual evolution.

Empower yourself by shifting focus from the obstacles to the blessings in your life.

LESSON

No matter what difficulty you are going through, if you can look at it through your divine spirit, you can appreciate it and grow from it.

WE ARE HERE FOR A REASON

The trees were a lush, deep, dark green. The clouds were white, puffy, and amazingly beautiful. The scenery reminded me of a postcard from a tropical island. Everything around me was simply breathtaking. The only sound that could be heard was the grinding that had just begun. Yes, out of nowhere, the brakes started making this obscene noise. Instantly I knew I was in trouble.

I stepped on the brake gently and it sounded like the bowels of hell opened. The brakes were grinding like something out of a *Nightmare on Elm Street* movie.

As I came upon a curve in the road, I slowed down and stepped gently on the brake. The car instantly went into a spin, crossing lanes and resting with a quick, hard thud against the bank on the other side of the road.

In the moments of the spin, I felt quite at ease. Believe me, I knew I was spinning, but my body was moving at a slower rate. My angels took the turn with me and helped me to gently go to the other side.

When the car stopped, my heart went into panic mode. My body shook and the tears stood at attention in my eyes. I was petrified. I quickly moved the car from the wrong side of the road and turned it around. It took me a few seconds, though it felt like minutes, to get out of the car.

My angels not only guided me and kept me from harm, they allowed my car to be safe as well. As I learn every day in my life, God can make the impossible possible. I walked out of the accident without a scratch. There was not a car in sight, even though it was rush hour, so I didn't hurt anyone else. And my car had nothing more than a lot of dirt on it. God is good.

As my heart and spirit began to merge again and my nerves calmed, I thought of my life spinning around in those thirty seconds. In those moments, I knew that we all tend to take life for granted. We have to realize that for every minute we are here we need to be thankful and appreciative. We need to realize that if we are still here on earth, not only are we blessed, we are here for a reason.

You are meant to fulfill some purpose for God. That is why you are still here. So listen to your spirit and stop taking your moments for granted.

If you were on your deathbed, you would cry, scream, shout, plead, beg, wish, hope, or pray for just one more moment of your life. You would hope that God would grant your wish and allow you a few more moments to live life to the fullest. You would pray that you had more time with loved ones and friends. Let's live that life now. Let's live a life where we can appreciate every breath, every friendship, every joy, every pain, every moment of our lives.

Our angels are with us. God is within us. We are powerful beings meant to make some things happen before we leave this earth.

LESSON

We need to realize that if we are still here on earth, not only are we blessed, we are here for a reason.

GOD'S TIME

Before you open your mouth to say it's taking too long for you to achieve your dream, take a second and ask yourself whose time line you are working with. Are you saying God is taking too long to give you what you want? That's exactly what you're saying if you start getting frustrated with your progress after God has already started to open some doors for you. If God is letting you in and showing you that you will achieve your dream, then you need to wait your turn. Continue to work on your dream every day and trust that your dream will be fulfilled when God says it's time.

We all get into the moments when we wonder what on earth is taking so long. It's almost as if we can grasp the dream but something is holding us back. For some reason, we can't achieve our dream in all its glory. The key is knowing that God never forgets you. God doesn't open up doors and then close them in your face. God doesn't give you a glimpse of your dream and then never provide you with a way to achieve it. My God doesn't work like that. Like fine art, we are being created and molded. We are being shaped and strengthened. We are being prepared for our greatness.

In these moments that feel like idleness, just know your time is coming. God is bringing you through and bringing you to your dream. It's just a matter of time, God's time.

LESSON

You will receive what you need in due time, God's time.

THE PATH TO A BETTER LIFE

The angels say that there are many ways we can live better lives. First we must learn to love. So many times we go through life without acknowledging our greatness, without appreciating how special and powerful we are, without appreciating that— we are created by God. We become so overwhelmed by life, childhood experiences, and emotional issues that we embrace a life filled with mistrust, insecurity, isolation, fear, and doubt. Many people start to view and live their lives based on the expectations that others have for them, and therefore, they can never find peace within themselves. The first step to happiness is love. Love yourself. Love your smile, your hair, your body, and your laugh.

The next level is forgiveness. On your journey to love, you must accept forgiveness. Forgiving others and yourself gives your spirit freedom.

The next step is creating a life of standards. In order to have a fulfilling life, you have to know what you really want and need. You have to be willing to make choices that empower you. You must fight for your life to be better, and stay away from relationships and situations that would allow you to remain stagnant. Be mindful of the choices you make each day.

Release the pain. The thing that holds so many people back in life is that they are living with pain. Pain can absorb your entire being. You must withdraw from living in pain. The goal is to go through the pain, not live in the pain.

Embrace life. Whatever you want, wants you. We live in an abundant universe. Whatever dreams you want to achieve can be achieved if you have the faith, determination, belief, and persistence to make it a reality.

Live in love. Instead of focusing on your personality and how people will perceive you, cultivate your spirit. When someone meets you, allow them to see your spirit shining through your eyes, living through your words, and existing in your actions. Allow your spirit to guide your life.

Believe in love. Eliminate all negative thoughts as soon as they appear. You must believe in the good of life and the good that exists within people. Your subconscious and conscious must want and expect the same things in order for you to receive what you really want. Make sure that your levels of thinking are consistent. Many times we may say we want something, but sabotage it by subconsciously thinking we will not get it, or that it is too difficult to achieve. Live a life of consistency.

Understand the power of your words. When you say "God is with me, I am blessed," you must embrace that with your entire spirit. You create your life each day by the words you speak and the choices you make. Be a conscious participant in your life. Be aware of your life, the patterns you are creating, and the changes you can make.

LESSON

Allow your spirit to guide your life.

ACKNOWLEDGE HOW POWERFUL YOU ARE

In truth, most people do not want to live a life they love. They actually do not think it is possible to love what they are doing. Many people focus on the problems in their life and ignore the solutions. But for those who dream of a better life, there are always choices and options. The people who can envision a better life have a more open mind and spirit. This allows them to make conscious choices for their life.

Living a life without regret is a daily decision. Each day you choose whether to react or act. You choose whom to allow into your life and whom to walk away from. You choose to do things that will fulfill you and satisfy your goals. You make decisions that will allow you to never look back in regret and say you would've, could've, or should've.

You have an inner strength that is far more powerful than any doubt or insecurity that could ever arise. So do not bathe in your stress. Instead, bask in the glow of knowing you have overcome many obstacles. Appreciate the lessons you have endured and the blessings that have been bestowed upon you.

Trust yourself. Love yourself. Cherish your spirit. Appreciate your strength. Acknowledge how powerful you are. Believe that you can create a life you love and then make it your reality.

LESSON

Living a life without regret is a daily decision.

Our days are numbered and our life is a gift. On our last day we will be remembered by: whom and how we loved; what we were willing to fight and live for; what we were capable of dealing with; and what we would not allow to be done to us.

On this day honor your strength, perseverance, courage, and love. Honor yourself. You are a precious gift.

THE WAY IT WAS INTENDED

There was a farmer who wanted to plant a seed. He found the best location where the sun would shine and the rain would reach the seed. He planted the seed and waited patiently for it to grow. He gave it whatever it needed. Eventually the seed began to grow and the farmer was happy.

He saw the first buds of the flower coming through the ground. He saw the flower emerge and begin to stretch. The farmer was amazed at the growth of the flower. Instead of being patient with the flower, as he was when it was a bud, he constantly stood over the flower to watch its growth. If the flower leaned to the left, he pulled it back into position. If the flower leaned forward or to the right, the farmer straightened it out.

Soon the farmer became frustrated with the growth of the flower. He went and got wiring and caged the flower in so that it could only go straight. After he fenced in the flower, something unexpected happened. The flower stopped growing.

The farmer came every day with food and water, but the flower would not grow. The farmer sank to the ground in despair. He knew this was meant to be a beautiful flower. It just wasn't doing what he wanted it to do. So he sighed and gave up. He took the wiring off the flower and walked away.

The farmer stayed away for days. He didn't want to see the flower as it died. After a few weeks, he returned to pluck the dead flower. But there before him was a strong flower sprouting with buds. Once the farmer had allowed the flower to grow on its own, it had surpassed his expectations.

LESSON

Know when to let go.

Release others from your expectations of them.

Allow your friends and child to be who they are destined to be.

We all have a spirit that can guide and protect us; we just need the ability and time to grow on our own.

Life doesn't always turn out the way we expected, it turns out the way it was intended.

THOSE WHO ARE READY

I used to be envious of people who never had to deal with being molested. I used to envy people who never had to deal with seeing a loved one on drugs. I used to envy people who never saw their father beat their mother. I used to think that their life was somehow better, more carefree. I used to think that they had it made. I used to think that their life was easier than mine. I used to think they were in a better place than I was.

What I know now is that for those of us who have endured painful things in our lives, we are a testament to the power of spirit. For those of us who have walked through hell and come out with a smile on our face, we are an example of the power of God's love.

For all of us who have fallen down, cried, and prayed for a way out and then realized that we could stand again and live again, we are powerful. So, although you may have endured some painful things, do not envy the lives of others. You do not know what their journey has been like. You do not have the same lessons to learn. You do not have the same spiritual endurance.

As you progress on your spiritual journey, you will find that the most enlightened, happy, and peaceful folks have been through a whole lot of things. I believe that God tests those who are ready to go to higher levels in their lives. He tests those who are able to rely on the strength of their spirit. He tests those who will help others by testifying about what they have gone through. In the end, it's not about how you were tested, but whether you were chosen to be tested at all. Thank God for acknowledging you. Thank God for knowing how strong you are.

Thank God for stretching you and allowing you to see the strength of your spirit.

LESSON

For those of us who have walked through hell and come out with a smile on our face, we are an example of the power of God's love.

WE ARE WORTHY

Every day so many of us live lives of quiet desperation. Each day many of us are afraid to step out and be who we are destined to be. The obstacles intimidate us. We limit our success to what we have seen friends and family achieve. We hold ourselves back from fulfillment because we are caught up in our day-to-day world. We have to stop this behavior.

Every day that you settle in an area of your life, you are slowly killing yourself. Every time you overlook some mistreatment by a friend, lover, or coworker, you are slowly giving a part of yourself away. You cannot live a life where you are settling and compromising who you are and what you stand for. You cannot allow just anyone to enter your world and become a part of it. Screen out the negativity. Find those who genuinely care for you and have your best interest in mind. Establish a life where you only receive the best. Set your expectations on receiving the best.

In the end, it's all about the choices we make. We can die slowly each day, or we can hold on to the fact that we are worthy. We are worthy to be loved, appreciated, adored, blessed, prosperous, happy, and fulfilled. We are worthy of greatness!

LESSON

Every day that you settle in an area of your life, you are slowly killing yourself.

PATIENCE IS A FORM OF FAITH

One of my ongoing battles has been acquiring patience. I am a truly impatient woman. As the years have gone by, though, I've continuously learned my lesson. I've learned that we all have to go through some things in order to learn from our life. And that is a blessing. Not everyone learns from his or her life. Not everyone sees his or her blessings. Not everyone acknowledges that God got him or her through the rough times.

Whenever there is a moment when you feel frustrated, whenever you feel that you just can't deal with a situation anymore, realize that in some way your spirit needs this. In some way, your spirit has to teach you something. Find the lesson. Wait patiently. The answers and solution will come.

Patience, I have learned, is simply a form of faith. As you rely on your faith, you must rely on your patience in order to get you through. The ability to truly rely on your patience and faith will allow you to see your life with clarity and understanding. These virtues will help you to make wise decisions and to appreciate the powerful being that you are. Patience will help you to see the hand of God move in your life.

LESSON

Patience is a form of faith.

GOD CANNOT BE TAKEN FROM YOU

———

Have you noticed that no matter where you are in life, there are people who will try to rob you of your positive energy?

I remember when I was in elementary school, the girls used to always taunt me with, "You think you're cute." In grade school, you really don't have a good comeback to that. All you know is that you want to make friends. It's only when we get older that we realize that these people saw something in us that they didn't see in themselves.

As we progress in life, we get to a place of certainty. Hopefully, we understand and appreciate where we are in life. We understand that we are powerful beings living spiritual lives, learning and growing every day.

At this point we know the thing that people are trying to steal is that positive energy. There are some people who just don't want to see that smile. Or hear your laugh. Or hear how good your life is going. There are some people who just cannot bear to hear about your good things. They are not your friends. They are more than just negative energy. They are a turning point for you. You can either fall into their belief system or you can assert your greatness.

Your power is never taken away from you. The God that is within you can never be taken away. But it can be given away. We can relinquish our power when we have insecurities and doubts. We can give others our power when we focus on the obstacles instead of our capabilities.

From this moment, when someone confronts you with their negative energy, I want you to embrace your spirituality. I want you to know that no one can take God from you. Dare someone to try. Dare them to try to take the essence from you. Dare them to take your joy. They cannot take God from you!

So on that day assert yourself, wear the vibe proudly, look that negative person in the eye. Tell them from your soul, "I dare you to try to take God from me." It's not a matter of words. Your eyes will tell it all.

LESSON

The God that is within you can never be taken away.

HOW DO WE BECOME EXTRAORDINARY?

———

Unhappiness lurks on the faces of people like a disease that cannot be cured. You can see the misery in their eyes. You can hear the pain in their voices, even when it's disguised as bitterness. You can look at someone and see the pain of life choices in their walk.

At this time in life so many of us are fighting to be more than what we have seen. We have dreams, hopes, and aspirations. How do we move beyond the norm and become extraordinary? How do we get the life that is well lived?

First we must truly want to have a better life. Then we must commit to creating it on all levels. We have to want happiness and fulfillment more than we are willing to deal with drama and pain. We have to make decisions that enhance our life and eliminate negativity. We have to get beyond wishful thinking and create strategies to make our lives better. We must fight with our spirit to live lives we love, rather than ones we want to run from.

As they say, love like you've never been hurt. Live life as though no one ever told you a negative word. Live your best life.

LESSON
Live life as though no one ever told you a negative word.

LIVE WITH TRUTH

The one thing that stops many of us from living lives we love is that we are fearful of the truth. We never want to confront it, speak it, or hear it.

The truth, though, will always become manifest. It's just a matter of time.

For so long I hid behind the truth because I didn't want to hurt someone's feelings. I didn't want to point out that they were not adding anything to my life. I never wanted to say the things that were embedded in my spirit.

How do we get past having good intentions and actually speak our truth? I've learned that the truth will come out in time. I've also realized that we can save ourselves so much time, energy, and emotional output if we simply speak our truth, live our truth, and be our truth.

I appreciate and admire honesty and truth. It takes courage and strength to speak it and stand behind it. In our lives, we have to make decisions each and every day. I believe with my heart that the most profound and authentic decision we can make is to be honest.

Be honest with yourself. Be honest with your needs and capabilities. Be honest with others. Empower yourself by living with truth.

LESSON

We can save ourselves so much time, energy, and emotional output if we simply speak our truth, live our truth, and be our truth.

YOU NEED TO DO SOMETHING

When it feels as though you are being held back from the good things life has to offer, when you feel as though something or someone is blocking your blessings, take a good look at yourself. Then take a good look at the people around you.

In order for God to give you the blessings he wants to bestow upon you, he needs you to do some things for him. Maybe you need to stop holding on to a painful relationship. Maybe you need to stop making excuses for a friendship that is not fulfilling you. Maybe you are living, working, or loving beneath your potential. Maybe God needs you to release it all so that he can give you what you need and deserve.

You are entitled to the blessings of life. You deserve to be happy and joyful. You deserve to live and give love. You deserve to have your spirit fulfilled. But you will not receive these things until you step out on faith and make changes in your life. Instead of the path of pain, dissatisfaction, unhappiness, and bitterness choose love, prosperity, hope, and faith. "Let Go, Let God" and you will receive your blessings.

LESSON

You cannot speak about or complain about change, you must make the necessary changes.

WHOM DO YOU CHERISH?

———

I had a conversation with a very good friend. She told me that her babysitter's mother had passed away. The woman was seventy-five years old and had died of a stroke. My friend, who is a powerful poet, was asked to write a poem for the service. So she wrote a poem and recited it at the service. After her reading, the minister asked if anyone would like to come up and say something about the deceased. No one came up. He explained that it didn't have to be anything profound. It could be something as simple as her smile or something about her that touched your life. No one came up.

It showed my friend and me that you have to be mindful of the impact you want to make on others. You have to be conscious of the type of legacy you leave behind. What type of memories do you want people to have of you?

To take it further, I suggested that a funeral also shows you which lives you cherish. Take the people you have in your life now. All the ones you call friends and the ones who would call you a friend (but whom you really regard as an associate). Suppose they passed away. You were on one coast and they were on another. Go down the list of people in your life and decide— honestly—whether you would attend their funeral or send a card to the family.

This is not based on whether you have the money to attend. This is whether your spirit tells you to attend or not. If you would not be there for someone's death, then why are they in your life now? Are they truly a friend or someone who just exists in your world?

LESSON

Establish and maintain friendships that you cherish.

YOU CANNOT BREAK ME

When I moved to Atlanta, I knew very few people. In fact, I only had one person I could call a friend. As life goes, when you are relying on someone, they will either be there for you or they will not. I have found that there is very seldom a middle ground.

So, with my need of his friendship and his knowledge of the city, I became somewhat vulnerable to him. When I became vulnerable, he became absent. His friendship was no longer present. He was no longer emotionally available. It was like dealing with a complete stranger. But it was worse because this person called himself my best friend. I thought he would be there for me to make my transition smooth. If anything, he made it one of the most challenging times of my life. And it was only a month of being "dependent" on him.

Sometimes I felt as though he were intentionally trying to break my spirit. I felt as though he were trying to see just how much I could put up with. He pushed our friendship to the limit. I was in so much pain. I was alone and afraid.

A lesson you will learn in life is that people do what they choose to do. They do not always do what you expect or need for them to do. Some people only think of their needs and never consider your needs or feelings.

You must strive to be a giver. To feel the joy God can give, you have to *give* in the essence of God. You have to give love in order to receive love. You can never give up on love because then you give up on God. God is love.

During those painful days, I wrote lessons in my journal. It was then that I wrote to remind myself that if God can talk through me, then no one has the power to break me.

No one has the ability to break down who and what you are unless you allow him or her to. They can hurt your feelings and even affect your spirit momentarily, but like Jesus said, you have to shake the dust off your feet and never return to a place that does not give your spirit peace.

Make a choice today to find strength and hope in yourself. If you are feeling alone, realize that God is with you every step of the way. God will never let you down. Just believe in him and he will get you through whatever torment is in your life. Just release all the pain, worry, and anxiety, and give it to God. He will take over and bring you to another level. Allow God to work in your life. He will eliminate the negatives and bring in the glory. He will bring you true friends, happiness, peace, and love. Believe me, I'm experiencing it all right now, and I wish the same for you.

Never give up hope. Never hold on to love. You need them both in order for your spirit to survive.

LESSON

People do one of two things—what they want to do and what you allow them to do.

WALK THROUGH FEAR

———

A few years ago, I was wondering why a relationship was not working out with a man I was dating. So I led him into a conversation to see what he would say about our situation. I remember he looked away from me and said, "Tasha, you're fearless. You don't need me for anything."

A lesson I have to pass on to you is, when someone tells you who they are, believe them. When someone says "You don't need me for anything," believe them. You may be caught up in a moment of love and confusion. They know that they are not adding anything to your life. They also know that they are incapable, or unwilling, to add anything to your life. The best thing you can do for your happiness is to always answer the question, "Is this person bringing me happiness or pain?" If anyone is constantly bringing you pain, they need to be eliminated from your life. They are detrimental to your emotional and spiritual well-being.

As far as him telling me I was fearless, I didn't believe him. I had the fear. I also had the courage to walk through that fear and pull it toward my destiny.

I believe that if we were constantly aware that God is within us and always with us, we would appreciate and love ourselves much more. We would represent ourselves from a position of power. No one would be able to define or limit who we are, or are capable of being. The power of our spirit would exude and show our strength without us ever uttering a word.

Always remember that you are a powerful being. You are a force to be reckoned with. God is within you, and when you are aware of that, there is no limit to what you can do.

LESSON

When someone tells you who they are, believe them.

IF YOU HAD NO FEAR

If you had no fear, who would you tell, "I love you?" If you had no fear, how would you change your life today? If you had no fear, what would you be able to say and do differently today? If today were your last day, what would you do to make an impact in someone's life?

Let's utilize the imagination. Take God's hand and walk through the fear. You are now empowered to do whatever will help your life become more fulfilled. You have the capability to achieve your dreams. You have the confidence, support, and motivation. You are able to stay on your path and walk toward your best life.

Imagine God saying, "Let's walk together. Keep moving toward your dream. Keep walking through the fear and you will get to your best life."

LESSON

Live your life as if fear did not exist.

The thing that you most want, you must be willing to give.

*Eliminate all negativity from your life so that when you
experience the positive things, you are able to fully enjoy them.
Allow yourself the pleasure of smiling from your soul.*

It is at the moment that we listen *to God, rather than talk to him, that we will receive the answers our soul needs.*

LIVE YOUR DREAMS

———

There was a man who began to plan his dream house. He had elaborate designs and intricate rooms. The house he envisioned was more beautiful than any he had ever seen. He could see it so clearly in his mind. He worked for days on creating the blueprint for his house.

His days became weeks, then months, then years. Time was passing him by, but he didn't notice it because he was so enthralled with the planning. He didn't realize that life was passing him by as well. In the time that had passed, he had never really stepped out and enjoyed life. His years had become consumed by his perpetual planning. Love, financial success, and true happiness had never found a place in his life. He had simply never made the time.

It was a devastating day when the man was found in his home. He had passed away in his sleep. All throughout his house there were plans, visions, and details for the dream house. He had never once lived his dream. And now he would never have the chance.

While life is about careful planning and choices, it is also about living. It is essential that we know what we want out of life. But it is equally important that we begin taking the steps to make those things happen.

LESSON

Don't allow yourself to get so caught up in your life that you plan it but never live it.

LIFE IS ABOUT CHOICES

Why are there some people who can make it through the storms of life, while some people remain in the downpour?

Life is about opening the spirit up to lessons. Everything we encounter in this lifetime is not only a choice but was requested by our spirit in order for us to experience growth. The unhappiness and dissatisfaction come into play when we do not listen to the needs of our spirit, or do not understand the lesson.

There are many people who will go to their grave holding on to all the painful things that have happened to them. I know that making it through painful life experiences is challenging. I understand what it's like to have your character and body assaulted. I understand what it's like to have a business fail and friendships end. I understand what it's like to have a parent or family member disappoint you terribly. I have learned, however, to keep walking, believing, and moving toward my freedom.

Early in my life, around age fourteen, I recognized that the problems of my parents were not my problems. The choices of my parents were not choices I would have to make later in life. I did not take responsibility for their life, nor did I fall into feeling like a victim because of what I have endured.

There are many people who will remain in the downpour of unhappiness because it is all they are choosing to know. We are all children of God, and therefore have the innate ability to experience joy and life to its fullest. Our choices are the only things that hold us back or move us forward.

When you hold on to painful memories from your childhood, you affect who you are today. As you hold on to negativity, you are never able to grasp all the positive blessings that want to come to you. When you hold on to bitterness, peace can never truly enter your heart. It saddens me to see people continue to make the same foolish and painful choices in their lives.

As a woman who has endured a lot, I will tell you this: Life is about choices. Make the choices that will lead to you having happiness. Be a conscious participant in your life. Look at the people you are allowing to come into your life. What type of energy do they bring with them?

Stop living in the storms of life and start moving toward happiness. Many times we learn lessons in painful ways, the key is to hold on to the lesson and release the pain.

LESSON

Our choices are the only things that hold us back or move us forward.

YOU ARE NOT PERFECT

———

There may have been some decisions you have had to make that have rocked you to your core, shaken your soul, and irritated your spirit. You may feel like you have just made the worst decision in the world. You may question your morals, standards, values, and decision-making. You may put yourself down and feel like you made foolish choices. The reality is, even in the midst of this, you are still in control.

You still have the ability to get through this. You have to know that you are making decisions based on what is best for you.

Do you realize that we can create our own illnesses? We get all these emotions trapped within our bodies and they have no outlet. We hold on to all this pain and it gets stored in our system. For your emotional, spiritual, and physical health, you have got to stop holding on to the past. You have got to stop judging yourself based on who you were in the past. The key question is, Who are you now? Who are you at this moment?

In the end, maybe you wouldn't make some of the same decisions you made in the past. But you know, Maya Angelou said it best, you made the best decision based on the information you had at the time.

You are not perfect. No one expects you to be perfect. You are a spiritual being who is here to learn lessons and go on a journey of this life. Make sure you learn the lesson and release yourself from the pain. Forgive yourself and give yourself your freedom.

LESSON

Pain can stop you. Fear can block you. The only thing that can set you free is love.

DO YOU HAVE MY BACK?

———

There's one thing I want to know
do you have my back
I mean do you have my back
when I'm up against a wall
and can't find a way out
will you pull me back
and help change my reality
when I'm on the flip side
and feeling good
will you be there then
will you have my back
I mean will you have my back

———

When I'm feeling like flying
because life is so good
will you smile and laugh with me
in my moment of joy
will you feel it like I feel it
will you experience the good with me too

what I've found to be true
is that there are so many who can be there in your bad times
they swim in your misery with you
tell you how bad life and people can be
but when things get good
they can't really hang
especially if life hasn't changed on their side
so what must be known clearly today is
can you hang
I mean do you have my back

———

Through the ups, the downs,
the good, the bad
will you be there when I need you
to hold me, hug me, laugh with me
cry with me, smile with me
will you be there with me through the moments of my life
or are you only picking certain times to be by my side
because what I want is
someone who is there with me through all the moments of
my life

———

So take a moment
think about it

like I'm thinking about it
and answer me honestly
if you can
from your spirit
from your soul
from your heart
do you have my back?

CHOOSE YOUR FRIENDS

Have you ever needed someone to be there for you and they simply didn't show up? They didn't call. They didn't say a word. And so, in your moment of need, you were left without the friend you thought had your back. The one thing we will all find out at some point in our lives is the difference between a friend and an acquaintance.

There are people who have been in our lives for years who are only acquaintances. It is not time nor professions of love that make a person your friend. A friend is someone who loves you during your good and bad moments. A friend upon hearing that you are sick will stop what they're doing and come to your side. When you are stepping out to live your dream, your friend will be there to watch you shine and to motivate you to keep going.

There are times in our lives when we will need the support of others. Sometimes all we need is the positive energy to surround us. It is at the moment your spirit needs something that you will find out who will really be there for you. It is so disappointing to find out that the people we call friends simply don't show up when we need them.

We have two choices in this situation. We can accept whatever excuse they give us or we can hold ourselves, and the friendships we wish to have, up to higher standards.

So many people are there with us during our painful moments. So many people have our backs when we are living in misery. But when our light begins to shine and our life begins to change, there are some people who simply will not be able to be there for us. Many of us make a choice not to call these people on their behavior because we are not willing to lose our "friend." The key is to know what you expect from a friend and to have standards for your relationships.

In order to have better friendships and relationships, we have to be willing to let go of mediocre relationships. We have to be willing to let go of the people who add nothing to our world. We need to be discerning in our choices of whom we extend our love, time, energy, and friendship too.

LESSON

In order to have better friendships and relationships, we have to be willing to let go of mediocre relationships.

YOU CAN'T FAKE THE FUNK

Remember that old saying, you can't fake the funk. Things could be going well. You could have a job that causes you no stress. You could be able to pay the bills, go out for a drink every now and then. You could be living a life without drama or tension. But still there is something tugging at your spirit, heart, and mind. There is something that's telling you that life is not perfect, that you are not living life to the fullest. And something is missing. So how do you define that something? How do you find out what you need in order to live a life less ordinary? How do you step out of the mundane and monotonous and start creating a life you love?

The first thing is to acknowledge your needs and feelings. You are not crazy for wanting or expecting more from your life. You are not irrational in thinking that you can create a better life for yourself. So you must realize that even when things appear "normal," you still may not be in the best situation for your overall happiness. So pay attention and acknowledge this feeling.

Then you must be willing to act on your feelings. How many people are able and willing to step out of the box? It is so amazing that people can live a life of misery, and when an opportunity arises, they find every reason why they should stay exactly where they are. Fear can cause you to remain stagnant and blocked. Fear can stop you from doing the things you love. So are you willing to believe that there is a better life for you?

Are you willing to walk away from the consistency of your life and see if you can actually love life? I often think of the slaves who followed Harriet Tubman. Many followed her simply because of faith, belief, and hope. There were also some who were just as miserable, but they decided not to leave the life they had. Why? Because they weren't willing to walk away from the familiar; they were afraid of the consequences. They thought man had more power over their life than God.

You are a powerful spiritual being who has a direct connection with God. God gives you the ideas, the courage, the strength, the faith, the hope, and the knowledge to achieve your dreams and live your life. If you feel that there is a better life for you, then you are absolutely right. You must know that you are embraced by angels. God has your back and you can live a better life. You can create a better life.

No matter how much you try, you can't fake the funk. You can't pretend to love life. Either you love it or you don't. And if you don't, you owe it to yourself, your spirit, your happiness, and God, to create a life you do love. Appreciate where you are, but work toward getting to where you really want to be in life.

LESSON

God gives you the ideas, the courage, the strength, the faith, the hope, and the knowledge to achieve your dreams and live your life.

Our expectations can be a limitation or the catalyst
to achieving a life we love.

The minute you stop searching, you will find that you are the source. Within your spirit, you have the answers to your problems, and the solutions to achieving your dreams.

YOU ARE WHOLE

———

For those who feel like there's a hole in their soul
what do you do
where do you begin
how do you find love and joy
you go within
peel back the layers
and see where the pain begins
study every year
examine every thought
look at what you have endured
experienced
and overcome
take away the bitterness
and make it strength
take away the anger
and give yourself freedom
look at the layers
and appreciate your life
listen to yourself breathe

and appreciate the force that sustains you

there is no hole

that cannot be filled by God

there is no void

that he cannot heal

but you must step forward

you must create another level of your life

you must go beyond your pain

and believe

just believe

in angels, in love, in healing, in God

believe

and change your life

fill yourself with love

and then

you will be filled

you will be healed

you will not be in search of things to fulfill you

or complete you

once you look at the layers

you will find

that you have been complete

the whole time

GO AROUND THE OBSTACLES

When we're in the car driving toward our destination, we can become irate if someone cuts us off or gets in our way. We feel frustrated if someone is in front of us, slowly making his or her way, and hindering us from moving along faster. As soon as the opportunity arises, we find a way to get around that person.

Wouldn't things be easier if we had the same courage and decision-making in our personal lives? How much better would life be if you immediately went around all the obstacles blocking your progress? How much closer to your dream would you be if you simply observed the situation, made a decision, and moved yourself closer to your destination (your dreams)?

LESSON

Stop living your life based on excuses and justifications, and by looking at the obstacles. Focus on your goals and dreams.

The one thing we know is that we are here for a moment.
We cannot control how long that moment will be,
but we can control what we do with the moments we have.

LET IT GO

Sometimes it is painful to look at a relationship and see the deterioration that will come. We often want to hold on to a belief that it will work out, that the person will change, or that the potential we see in them will suddenly become manifest. These relationships are similar to a snake shedding its skin. Though it may be comfortable and familiar, it must be removed so that a better life can begin.

Just as we strive to nurture our body, we should focus on giving our spirit what it needs—love, friendship, and positive energy.

LESSON

You can limit your life and possibilities by holding on to people and places from the past that are not meant to be a part of your future.

WHAT DO YOU WANT TO SEE?

———

Two men walked down the same road for years, but they never lived the same life or saw the same things. One man saw only what his mind could believe, while the other man saw the journey through his spirit and lived a better life.

It is not about what path you take, how many experiences you have endured, how people have treated you; it is about the life you are willing to create.

Though there may have been pain, are you willing to believe in joy?

Though there may have been heartache, are you willing to believe in love?

Though you may have seen poverty, are you willing to believe in wealth?

Though your spirit may have suffered, are you willing to believe that you can be restored?

The only person who can break you is you. The only person who can stop you from achieving a dream is you. The only person who can ever stop you from living a life you love is you. So be willing to believe in things the masses cannot believe. Be willing to believe that you deserve the best. Be willing to believe that your dreams will become a reality.

Do not allow your life to be broken by negative spirits and people. Rise above it all and live a life worth living again. Live the life of your dreams.

LESSON

The only person who can ever stop you from living a life you love is you.

Just because someone can kneel in the form of prayer does not mean they are actually listening to God.

Every cry to God does not go unanswered; there are just some things God knows you shouldn't be crying over.

Life cannot improve or change without someone making the commitment to make the change.

FORGIVING IS POWER

We were running late for school and I had to tie my shoe. I told my friends to keep walking and I'd catch up. I bent down to tie my shoe and instantly there were two other shoes in front of me, facing me. I looked up slowly and there was a man who simply said, "Get up." I looked past him and could not see my friends. I couldn't see the security guard who helped us cross the street. All I could see was my apartment complex behind me, a bridge to the right, park to the left, and this tall Black man in front of me. I don't remember how he took me under the bridge. I don't know whether he pulled me, covered my mouth, or if I simply cried and followed. I don't remember trying to run. I simply remember his words: "Scream and I will kill you. And when I let you go, if you tell anyone, I will kill your mother and father." It was those words that bought my years of silence.

I never said a word. I cried that day, arrived at school late, and then tuned out the whole thing until it came flashing back nearly ten years later.

I drove up to the bridge and looked at the same sights I saw that day. Because of that man, I had acquired a great fear of being in a park, driving in a park, sitting in a park. The sight of so many trees overwhelmed me. I was afraid to be that alone in a space where no one can hear and no one can really see. I was intimidated by the great spaces of the park. That man had robbed me of the joy of seeing the trees. He robbed me of smelling flowers and swinging in the park. He had taken my childhood and left me with the fear that my words could kill my parents. But today I was back.

I held on to the bridge for dear life and inhaled and exhaled. I was letting go. Letting go of the pain, the hurt, the fear, the anger, the rage, and the unhappiness. I closed my eyes, inhaled and exhaled, and took my strength back. With my eyes closed, I saw her. She was only five, going on six, and had stopped to tie her shoe. When she looked up, she smiled at me and I smiled back. She had two ponytails and a puffy yellow coat. She stretched out her hand and I hesitated. I wanted my childhood back so desperately but was afraid I had lost all chances of regaining that innocence. She stood up then and looked me in my eyes. "I'm okay now," she said. "I'm still here. He didn't take me away. I'm right here." She smiled. "I'm right here," she said again, and took my hand. I looked at her and I cried and embraced the childhood I thought had been taken away from me. I cried harder and my tears fell on the bridge and I felt her hand slip from mine. And I was restored. That little girl that I thought I had disappointed and lost for good was still there. She wasn't angry. She wasn't bitter. She was just waiting for me to find her again. I embraced her within me and looked around again.

This time I could see it. I could see the beauty of the trees. I could see the children laughing. I could see the puffy white clouds above me. I breathed in and inhaled my power. I reclaimed my life and left all the unhappy moments right there on that bridge.

I will never forget what that strange man did to me, but I no longer live with it. And though he was never found so that he could be held accountable for his crime, I know with all my heart and spirit that the day I let go was the day I set myself free and the day he was left alone to remember the pain he caused a small child.

LESSON

Forgiveness is a power we can give to ourselves. When we forgive, we are restored. When we forgive, we take back our strength. When we forgive, we set ourselves free.

THE JOURNEY OF YOUR LIFE

———

There was a young woman who was walking through the forest. Her spirit was well. She was content, though not in love with her life. She could see the beauty around her and wanted to live a life in which she could appreciate that beauty all the time. She continued walking. The path began to twist. The sky instantly turned stormy gray. There was darkness beginning to appear around her. The young woman became somewhat frightened and unsure of where she was going. Though she knew she was walking in the right direction, it just no longer felt right. Her heart began to race. She called out to God, and then her foot slipped.

She was suddenly submerged in what felt like murky water. Her spirit felt heavy and tears formed in her eyes. She prayed and wondered how her life had changed so quickly. What had gone wrong? The young woman tried to calm herself. I can get through this, she said to herself. This will pass.

She moved her arms and thought that she was not making progress. She was not moving forward or backward. She seemed to be stuck in one position. It now felt like she was in quicksand, taking meaningless steps. She shut her eyes and prayed again. God, I need you.

She felt a warm feeling on her face and then her spirit felt light. She could breathe easy again. Her eyes opened and the rays of the sun hit her eyes. For some reason she smiled and tried to step up.

Amazingly, she felt her foot hit solid ground. She could move. She really could get out of this pit. As she climbed up and out of the rut, a voice spoke to her.

There is always calm before the storm. In order to bring you closer to me, you have to go through some things. In order to make your life better, you have to see how low it can go. Then you may appreciate your strength, courage, and faith when you come out of it. You always have the ability to change your life because God is with you. You are never alone. You have never taken a wrong step in the journey of your life. God is always right here with you to push you up or pull you out.

Though you may feel like life is stagnant or that you're not making as much progress as you would like, just know that God has your back. Things will be revealed to you when your spirit is ready for them. As long as you continue to learn and grow from your life, you are never in the same position. You are always moving forward and moving closer to God.

LESSON

You always have the ability to change your life.

SCREAMING IN MY HEART

All my baby daughter had to do was make it up the steps to unlock the door and retrieve her book bag. But there were huge bumblebees in her way. Needless to say, she was walking on shaky legs. I watched as she hesitated momentarily and then ascended up the steps and into the house. Once she started walking, she never stopped.

I watched in amazement as my little seven-year-old, who is afraid of bees, made it back to the car and sat down. Then she answered the question I had in my thoughts. "You know, Mommy, I was screaming in my heart, but I couldn't let it show, and I had to keep going anyway. How else would I get what I wanted?"

How do you respond to that?

The questions for the moment are: Do you have the same amount of courage as you did as a child? Remember when you could easily climb a tree and turn a mud pie into apple pie? Remember when your imagination took you wherever you wanted to be and dreams always came true?

What happened?

Are you stuck in the zone? You know, the analysis paralysis zone. I am all too familiar with that zone. I could describe how it feels to live there, dream there, and get stuck there. But I know you already know what it feels like to be stagnant. I know you know what it feels like to have a dream in your head that you desperately want to see become reality. But how do you find the time to live your dream life when you've gotten caught up in the "real world"?

I TRULY believe that when God gives you a vision, the only thing you have to do is pursue it with your spirit and with your heart. You cannot look at obstacles, objections, excuses, or limitations. You are not taking this walk alone. God gave you the vision, and for that reason, there is NOTHING that can stop you from achieving it except you.

I choose to no longer be my own worst enemy. I choose to stop thinking I'm stuck in life. I choose to LIVE my life now, today, in this moment and on my terms.

At moments in our lives, we can all become stuck. Many of us have achieved great things, yet we still put ourselves down for not doing more, for not doing enough. Many of us are able to maintain our sanity in spite of living in the worst of circumstances, yet we still never give ourselves credit for surviving with our spirit and heart intact. Many of us dream big, but we never allow ourselves the time to take the steps toward achieving these dreams. Instead, we keep our dreams locked in our hearts and our heads. We never share our spirit because "life is about more than fulfilling dreams." I disagree, spirits. Life is all about fulfilling dreams.

Hear me loud and clear—there is no more trying. There are no more *gonna's*—gonna see, gonna try. *Gonna* is dead, and trying does not exist. In this moment, you must do what needs to be done.

Stop living life halfway. Live it to the fullest.

I know you know you are blessed. I know you know that God loves you. You know that you're precious, and special, and beautiful, and talented, and gifted. You know that you are here for a purpose. And it is time to start living your life on purpose.

We must stop saying that we don't know what to do. If we took the time to simply get still and listen, our spirit would tell us what to do. The answers are all within, we just have to be ready to listen and take action.

LESSON

The only way to get what you want is to stay focused and keep walking toward your goal.

"It's amazing how we condemn ourselves to lives of desperation without fighting to be free."
—*Darnella Ford, author*

LIFE IS ABOUT TIMING

———

Life is about timing. When it is your time to shine, you will shine. There is a light that has been stored in your soul by God, and when the moment comes, it will be released. We have to realize that there are gifts and talents within our spirit. These are the blessings that we are to share with the world in order to receive our blessing.

Don't become impatient or frustrated with yourself or your progress. Sometimes the right moments are still being created and you're just not ready yet. Trust your spirit and trust God, your time is coming. Continue to have faith, believe in yourself, and keep pushing toward making your dreams a reality.

LESSON

There is a light that has been stored in your soul by God, and when the moment comes, it will be released.

Once you are able to give what you want,
you will receive what you need.

FOUR THOUGHTS WE NEED

So many times in my life I have encountered problems and immediately become worried, anxious, stressed, and frustrated. So many times I wondered how on earth I would get myself out of a situation. I sat and thought about the many problems God has solved for me. I could see God's hand in everything he brought me through. I appreciated the lessons, received many blessings, and became a better spirit. So when situations hit me now, I know that God has control. I don't have to temporarily lose my mind. My spirit stays still, my mind stays focused, and I listen to the words of God. Then I take action.

LESSON

When you encounter a situation, obstacle, or problem, you must remember:

Everything happens for a reason
There is a lesson to be taught
God will get me through
This too shall pass

These four thoughts must be embedded into your mind and spirit. They must become part of your belief system. They will help you to make wise decisions.

SILLY ME

———

Silly me

I've been saying woe is me

overlooking the fact that I can get up and breathe

Silly me

I'm complaining about where my life is going

but forgetting that I'm blessed with the ability to walk

Silly me

I keep wondering whether I'll really achieve my dreams

not realizing that whatever God gave me will become manifest

Silly me for having faith only after the fact

when I need to know that GOD is always with me

Silly me for ever doubting myself, for questioning my

judgment, for being afraid

Silly me, I am powerful and I keep forgetting

Silly me

Silly me

Silly me

I am powerful

I am a child of God

I am blessed

I will stop being so silly

I VOW

———

I vow that whenever I am hurt
I will tell you why
I vow that whenever I feel confused
I will ask for help
I vow to remember that you are a child of God
a friend of mine
a spirit that I have a connection with
and I will treat you as though I love you
and I ask that you do the same for me
talk to me, share with me, cry with me, laugh with me
be yourself with me
I vow to be the best friend possible
I vow to be there when you really need me
I vow to appreciate the moments of my life
I promise to disregard the moments
when words are said in anger
and look beneath to your true intention
and the love that is there
I promise to share my love

and be love
I promise to never forget the lives that have touched me
and pray that I touch the lives of others
I vow to never forget that life is precious
that moments are precious
I vow to remember that I am always leaving an impression
and so I commit to letting you know that above all else
you are loved
you are loved
and wherever I am
you are in my heart and in my thoughts

DON'T WAIT UNTIL IT'S TOO LATE

———

Although we haven't stepped out on faith and used our talents, somehow we know they will not leave us. But what if they did? What if one day you woke up without the ability to do the special things you can do now? What if you were never given the chance to use your talents again? What if you had waited too long and now someone else had your talents?

We have to know that God gave us everything for a reason. Our talents are our blessings. Our talents are the things that will help us to have that life we so desperately want. We just have to believe and use our gifts. Don't take your talents for granted. Find ways to use your talent every day.

LESSON

Share your talents with the world; it is the way you leave an impression of your soul.

IN THE BLINK OF AN EYE

In the blink of an eye, you can lose your chance to say what's in your heart.

In the blink of an eye, you can become fearful of achieving your dreams.

In the blink of an eye, you can say the wrong thing and damage someone's soul.

In the blink of an eye, you will lose moments of your life.

In the blink of an eye, you can create life.

In the blink of an eye, you can make the decision to be truthful, to live fully, to be your best self.

In the blink of an eye, you can decide to love yourself and love your life.

In the blink of an eye, you can share your joy or pain.

In the blink of an eye, you can make someone smile or laugh.

In the blink of an eye, you can change a life.

In the blink of an eye, you can embrace God in your life.

In the blink of an eye, you can choose your emotions.

In the blink of an eye, you can choose to be wealthy.

In the blink of an eye, you can be healed.

In the blink of an eye, you can forgive.

Every day we wake up with the ability to do our heart's desire. But somewhere between the moment of our eyes opening and our feet hitting the floor, we tend to forget our dreams. We leave our lives we love in our slumber, and arise to live a life we tolerate—at best. It is time to change some things.

When will it be your moment to live from your heart? When will it be your moment to give and receive love? When will it be your moment to laugh out loud, cry hard, and live life on your terms?

You have it all inside of you. In the blink of an eye, you can be free. Everything you need to change your life is with you right now. In the blink of an eye, you can make a decision to change your life.

The question is, when will you get tired of holding yourself back? When will enough be enough? Somewhere within you there is a thought that you can't do something. You are limiting yourself. And when you limit yourself, you limit the possibilities of God to work through you. You have to believe with all your heart and soul that the God that created you instilled greatness in you. And the world is waiting for it to come out.

The world is waiting to receive your talents. The world is waiting to receive the unique voice and spirit that comprises you. We are waiting for you to realize that you are meant to live fully. We are waiting for you to release yourself from pain and embrace love. We are waiting for you to get out of the fear zone and know that every step you take is blessed by an angel. We are waiting for you to realize your power because we need it, just as much as you need it. You are needed. You are needed. Bring your talent out. Share your greatness with the world.

In the blink of an eye, you can change your world by just thinking differently.

LESSON

Don't miss out on the joy of life because you were too afraid to take a chance. Don't miss out on love because you were too afraid to speak up. Don't miss out on living life because you were too afraid to take a chance. Use the moments that you are given, to create your best life.

Happiness is the thing we lose every day
that we choose to deal with negative people and situations.
Happiness is not something you have to find, it is
something you choose to experience.

DON'T TAKE YOURSELF FOR GRANTED

So many times in life we take ourselves for granted. We take our kindness, our talent, our laughter, and our love for granted. And instead of realizing how precious those things are, and how precious we are, we focus on the negativity. We focus on a bad day, a bad job, or a bad relationship. We let the negativity overwhelm us to the point where we can no longer see the positive things in our lives. We take the fact that we have a home, food, clothing, and health for granted. We take the fact that we're still on this earth for granted. We have to realize that who we are is so special to God. We have to focus in on that "specialness" and appreciate it. Appreciate yourself. Love yourself. Give to yourself as you would give to others.

So many times we give more to other people than we give to ourselves. Do you realize that if a friend is in a bad mood you'll be there with encouragement? If someone is unhappy in their job, you'll counsel them and tell them it's going to be all right, that they deserve better, and that they will get it. But how often do you tell yourself you are special? How often do you tell yourself that you are powerful, beautiful, loving, and strong?

Can you make the time today to acknowledge yourself? Just say thank you to yourself for overcoming obstacles and living life. Thank yourself for being the precious person that you are.

You are so worth it.

LESSON

Thank yourself for being the precious person that you are.

THE CHOICES THAT AFFECT OUR LIVES

It is so disheartening to see people who never understood the power they possessed. Sometimes misery lies just behind their eyes and you see the pain of bad choices and memories. It is difficult to look someone in the eye and know within seconds that their life has been painful. You know instantly by someone's spirit whether they have been through painful periods of their lives and never recovered.

I wish for so many people to be able to have the joy of life in their eyes. I wish to have it consistently myself.

It becomes clear every day that we make the choices that affect our lives. Every day we wake up with the power to change our lives. Every day we wake up with the ability to make a new start. We need to use the time we have to create the life we want. Let our souls shine through our eyes and through our smile.

Be honest and sincere about what you want out of life and accept nothing less. Be consistent with the values and standards you have, and uphold them in your personal and professional life. Make a commitment to yourself to enjoy life. Make a commitment to eliminate negative energy from your life. Get past the point of tolerating and settling in relationships and your career. Step out on faith and know that what your heart desires and needs, God will provide for you.

LESSON

Be honest and sincere about what you want out of life and accept nothing less. Be consistent with the values and standards you have and uphold them in your personal and professional life.

THREE PHRASES THAT HURT YOUR SPIRIT

———

There are three phrases that will hurt your spirit and make you cry: *I Could Have, I Would Have,* or *I Should Have.* I could have ended this relationship a lot sooner. I could have gone back to get my degree. I could have done this and I could have done that. Saying *I could have* will damage your soul. As I go through my lessons in life, one thing my angels have shared with me is that we all need to eliminate the phrase *I could have* from our mental thoughts. Eliminate it from your vocabulary. As spirits and children of God, we have to realize that everything happens for a reason, and it happens in God's time. Be grateful for the hindsight and wisdom you have acquired along the way, but never beat yourself up with the words *I could have.* You can be certain, if it was not the will of God, there is no way you could have.

Always remember that you are a vessel of God. When you are ready to receive the lesson, you will receive it. When your spirit is ready to make life-changing choices, you will make them. God knows the difference between what you say from your mouth and what you say from your spirit.

LESSON

The only way you can achieve things in life is if your spirit and mouth are saying and wanting the same thing.

EXHALE

When *Waiting to Exhale* debuted, I was too young to fully understand what they meant by just wanting to exhale. But as you get older, you realize that there are times in your life when you simply breathe out the negativity and inhale the positive energy. Have you ever released someone from your life and felt immediately empowered? You felt as though a weight had been lifted from your shoulders? Like a burden had been removed? Whew, those are the moments when you know you just made the best choice for your spiritual growth and life. Those are the moments when you know you just got a "blessing-blocker" out of your life.

As I continue on my spiritual journey, I realize how powerful God made us. He equipped us with the essentials to live a life we love. We have many gifts; two important ones are truth and spirit. If we live our life based on our truth, we will make the best choices for our lives. We will not settle and we will not compromise when it comes to our values, morals, and standards. When we live in truth, we have no choice but to pursue everything our spirit desires. When we live in truth, we can only have fulfilling relationships because we will accept nothing less. When we live in truth, we will never allow anyone to block our blessings. We won't allow negativity or drama to affect our lives.

The next gift is our spirit. If we took the time to listen to the needs of our spirit, we would live better lives. Our spirit always tells us what is right for us, what is best for us. Our spirit is our direct connection to the powerful forces that work on our behalf. The key is knowing when to exhale. Just know when to let go.

LESSON

Live in truth and honor the needs of your spirit.

There must be balance between our ego and our truth.
We must know if we are fighting for something because our ego
wants it or because our spirit needs it.

BE CAREFUL WHAT YOU
PRAY FOR

How many times have you prayed to receive something and then gotten anxious when you received it? It seems as though we have no problem praying for an answer or solution, but when God provides it, we are not always willing to accept it.

I was in a relationship that was going nowhere. I prayed and prayed to God to please let it work out. The answer I always received was: "Be careful what you pray for because you just might get it." I pretended as though that made no sense to me and continued to pray for this man, who did not love himself, to love me. It was of course useless.

Once that so-called energy of love evaporated I got to see this man for who he really was. It was then that I thanked God for not giving me this man when I had wanted him so desperately. I thanked God for giving me what I needed and not what I wanted. It was a blessing.

Our prayers are always answered. We just may not receive the answer we had wanted. Listen and accept what God tells you. This will help you to avoid drama and receive your blessings.

LESSON

Be careful what you pray for—you just might get it.

FINDING PROSPERITY

Have you ever been a step above just getting by and wondered why you were not prosperous? You wondered why you had not obtained wealth or achieved your dream? Does this step in your life frustrate you?

In this situation we have to focus on a few things. First, are you doing enough? Are you doing everything you can to change the status of your life? Are you going to bed tired because you pushed yourself to the limits so that you could achieve your dream? You should not enter into sleep at night until you have done something, even one thing, to improve your life.

Second, have you defined your success? The best thing we can do is realize that success is a journey. Each day that you acquire a new skill, complete another task, or dream bigger, you are successful. When you can see the growth in your spirit and intellect, you are successful. When you know that you are a better person today than you were yesterday, you are successful. When you love and like yourself exactly the way you are, you are successful.

Third, we must realize that prosperity does not come to those who are idle. Prosperity comes to those who hustle and push their dream into existence. Prosperity comes to those who refuse to settle and become complacent.

LESSON
Prosperity comes to those who seek it.

CAN YOU SPEAK YOUR TRUTH?

There are so many people who live lives of quiet desperation, wallowing in depression, searching for someone or something to bring them out of the funk. If we simply had the ability to be truthful about our lives, without fear of judgment and condescending remarks, wouldn't we share ourselves with one another? Wouldn't we tell it like it really is, rather than how it's supposed to be? Wouldn't we be more willing to cry, scream, and shout with one another? Wouldn't we be more honest about how we feel about our life if we knew we had the support and faith of others?

There is always someone who can relate to what you're going through. There is always someone who can understand the pain, frustration, and fear. There is always something that can guide you back to happiness and fulfillment. There is something or someone that can help you feel peace in your heart and have a smile on your face. Don't ever give up. Don't ever sink into despair. It's all right to be frustrated. It's okay to cry. It's okay to experience your emotions, but don't let them overcome you.

Today is the day you have to be honest with yourself. Are you where you want to be? Did you plan to be where you are now? If you didn't plan, if you're not happy, then make a plan today. Make a way out of unhappiness and go toward joy. It's right there. Just reach out and take your blessings. Grab your joy. You deserve it.

LESSON

Be honest.

THINGS WILL WORK OUT

———

Every morning most of us take something for granted. As we inhale and exhale, we never appreciate the strength of our lungs. We never appreciate the capability of our body to carry us forward, to help us see, think, and feel. Instead, we assume that these will be handled naturally. But when it comes to our worries and stress over money, jobs, friendships, and relationships, we wonder how we will handle things. My question is, If God is giving you what you need in order for your body to function, won't he give you what you need in order for your life to function?

As much as we trust that our next breath will flow, we need to trust that God will provide for our spirit as well. The greatest lesson to learn in life is that you are not alone. You are never alone. You are never forgotten. No problem is ever too much for you to bear. No struggle is too difficult for you to overcome.

In order to appreciate something, you must be still. You must release yourself from being anxious and worrying. You must know that what seems overwhelming to you is minor to God. Just know that God wants your life to flow just like those breaths you take for granted every morning.

LESSON

Things will always work out.

AT THIS MOMENT

So many people live their lives based on the past. So many are haunted by the things they did a few years ago. Many are haunted by the things they did last night or last week. The best thing we can do is release ourselves from the pain of memories. Release yourself from the expectations you had of yourself in that moment. Live for this moment.

In this moment, with the person you are today, what are your expectations? What do you love about yourself? What have you learned from your life?

We will be blessed with peace and happiness when we are able to forgive ourselves and move forward. So many times in life the only thing holding us back from success and love is ourselves. Let yourself go! Let go of the past and claim your future. Forgive yourself for any indiscretion or pain you may have caused another person. Allow yourself to grow and live life without obstacles.

THIS IS YOUR COMMITMENT FOR LIFE:

It was not in the second that I did the act, nor the minute that I knew better. It was in the minute that I committed to living a better life that forgiveness was given to myself. I love myself enough to acknowledge the pain, the lesson, and the blessing of learning from my life.

You cannot judge me based on my yesterday. You cannot judge me based on the promise of my tomorrow. Everything I can offer—the pureness of my heart, my spirit, my soul, my love, my friendship, and my life—is offered to you today. So if you must judge me, then judge the person I am at this moment.

For at this moment I am a child of God. At this moment, I am powerful. At this moment I am free. So love who I am TO-DAY. Just as I love myself today.

You are beautiful today. You are forgiven today. You are loved today. Give yourself the freedom you deserve and choose to live a life of happiness.

SPIRITUAL LESSONS

THE COMPLETE LIST

1. Life changes when you commit to doing what is necessary to create a life you love.
2. Each day write down the reasons you should be grateful and the goals that make living your life worthwhile.
3. You are powerful, and people must be worthy to be in the presence of the God that exists within you.
4. People do not just lie to you; you allow them to lie to you.
5. We always know when something is right for us or not. We just tend not to listen to the truth our spirit tells us.
6. If you want love, you must give love.
   If you want faith, you must have faith in others.
   If you want to believe in the good of others, you must be good.
   If you want to trust again, you must be trustworthy.
   If you want success, you must help others.

7. Never misuse your time, energy, or love.

8. Our best advice comes from our most powerful connection to God, our intuition.

9. You are not the only one who has experienced pain, but you can be one of the few to get over it and make your life glorious.

10. You cannot move forward if there are energies in your life that are holding you back.

11. When spirit touches your heart, soul, and mind and directs you to eliminate some folks from your life, you need to listen and take action.

12. If you choose to live a life of mediocrity, then you will always settle in some area of your life. It is those who push toward greatness who will expect, receive, and give only the best in everything they do.

13. It is easier to plan for a dream than it is to walk in the path of the dream and endure the journey.

14. Make your life stand for something. Leave a legacy.

15. If you are truly sick and tired of the way your life is flowing, change the direction. Change! Stop talking about it. Stop hoping for it and simply make the changes. Take the first step toward your destiny.

16. Love the life you live.

17. God has got your back, and there is not a person in this world who can block your blessings except you.

18. There are times in your life when you will want to give up. You cannot fall victim to your life. Failure is not an option.

19. No person can take God away from you. And if they can-

not take away the God that exists within you, then they can never take away who you are. They can never take your soul and spirit unless you give it away.

20. The biggest obstacles we face are the ones that dwell in our minds.

21. At the worst possible moment, you will find out who is your friend and who is not. Thank God for showing you, then make a decision to get all the negative energy out of your life.

22. Life is about choice. We are all given a choice every day to choose love or fear, happiness or pain, wealth or poverty.

23. Courage is the ability to feel fear in your heart and still keep moving.

24. Listen to your life. It will show you who you are and where you are headed.

25. Never allow anyone to hold you back in any way.

26. The answers lie within; all you have to do is ask.

27. Appreciate your life; it's God's gift to you.

28. Commit to your happiness.

29. We limit ourselves from living a life of happiness because we are afraid to make changes.

30. Treat others the same way you would want God to treat you—with love!

31. Love never has and never will make you become less than you are intended to become.

32. We can all change the world; it's the only way true change is made—one person at a time.

33. Commit to living a better life, and create the circumstances to make your dreams reality.

34. Every time you call on God, you gain the opportunity to grow closer to him.

35. Give what you want, do not expect it in return, and you will be blessed.

36. No matter what difficulty you are going through, if you can look at it through your divine spirit, you can appreciate it and grow from it.

37. We need to realize that if we are still here on earth, not only are we blessed, we are here for a reason.

38. You will receive what you need in due time, God's time.

39. Allow your spirit to guide your life.

40. Living a life without regret is a daily decision.

41. Know when to let go.
    Release others from your expectations of them.
    Allow your friends and child to be who they are destined to be.
    We all have a spirit that can guide and protect us; we just need the ability and time to grow on our own.
    Life doesn't always turn out the way we expected, it turns out the way it was intended.

42. For those of us who have walked through hell and come out with a smile on our face, we are an example of the power of God's love.

43. Every day that you settle in an area of your life, you are slowly killing yourself.

44. Patience is a form of faith.

45. The God that is within you can never be taken away.

46. Live life as though no one ever told you a negative word.

47. We can save ourselves so much time, energy, and emo-

tional output if we simply speak our truth, live our truth, and be our truth.

48. You cannot speak about or complain about change, you must make the necessary changes.

49. Establish and maintain friendships that you cherish.

50. People do one of two things—what they want to do and what you allow them to do.

51. When someone tells you who they are, believe them.

52. Life your life as if fear did not exist.

53. Don't allow yourself to get so caught up in your life that you plan it but never live it.

54. Our choices are the only things that hold us back or move us forward.

55. Pain can stop you. Fear can block you. The only thing that can set you free is love.

56. In order to have better friendships and relationships, we have to be willing to let go of mediocre relationships.

57. God gives you the ideas, the courage, the strength, the faith, the hope, and the knowledge to achieve your dreams and live your life.

58. Stop living your life based on excuses and justifications, and by looking at the obstacles. Focus on your goals and dreams.

59. You can limit your life and possibilities by holding on to people and places from the past that are not meant to be a part of your future.

60. The only person who can ever stop you from living a life you love is you.

61. Forgiveness is a power we can give to ourselves. When we

forgive, we are restored. When we forgive, we take back our strength. When we forgive, we set ourselves free.

62. You always have the ability to change your life.

63. The only way to get what you want is to stay focused and keep walking toward your goal.

64. There is a light that has been stored in your soul by God, and when the moment comes, it will be released.

65. When you encounter a situation, obstacle, or problem, you must remember:
    Everything happens for a reason
    There is a lesson to be taught
    God will get me through
    This too shall pass

66. Share your talents with the world; it is the way you leave an impression of your soul.

67. Don't miss out on the joy of life because you were too afraid to take a chance. Don't miss out on love because you were too afraid to speak up. Don't miss out on living life because you were too afraid to take a chance. Use the moments that you are given, to create your best life.

68. Thank yourself for being the precious person that you are.

69. Be honest and sincere about what you want out of life and accept nothing less. Be consistent with the values and standards you have and uphold them in your personal and professional life.

70. The only way you can achieve things in life is if your spirit and mouth are saying and wanting the same thing.

71. Live in truth and honor the needs of your spirit.

72. Be careful what you pray for—you just might get it.
73. Prosperity comes to those who seek it.
74. Be honest.
75. Things will always work out.